SpringerBriefs in Law

More information about this series at http://www.springer.com/series/10164

María de Miguel Molina
Virginia Santamarina Campos
Editors

Ethics and Civil Drones

European Policies and Proposals
for the Industry

Editors
María de Miguel Molina
Department of Management
Polytechnic University of Valencia
Valencia
Spain

Virginia Santamarina Campos
Conservation and Restoration of Cultural
  Heritage
Polytechnic University of Valencia
Valencia
Spain

ISSN 2192-855X   ISSN 2192-8568   (electronic)
SpringerBriefs in Law
ISBN 978-3-319-71086-0   ISBN 978-3-319-71087-7   (eBook)
https://doi.org/10.1007/978-3-319-71087-7

Library of Congress Control Number: 2017959312

Printed on acid-free paper

This Springer imprint is published by Springer Nature
The registered company is Springer International Publishing AG
The registered company address is: Gewerbestrasse 11, 6330 Cham, Switzerland

Foreword

Aviation has come a long way since the Montgolfier brothers carried out the first free flight of a hot air balloon across Paris in 1783. It took a further 120 years before the Wright brothers achieved sustained controlled powered flight in 1903. Not too long after that, the first scheduled commercial air passenger flight took off in 1914 across Tampa Bay, Florida. The aviation sector has seen tremendous advances both in relation to the technology and volume of air traffic since that first commercial flight. Whilst the civil aviation section generally has relied on human piloted air-crafts, unmanned 'pilotless' drones have also been developing alongside, albeit at a much smaller scale. Until the not too distant past, the uses of drones have been mainly confined to military and surveillance purposes. The significance of drones has, however, increased substantially in the recent years in the light of its use in various other sectors including agriculture, inspection, media and entertainment, as well as by hobbyists. It will only be a matter of time before remotely piloted aircrafts enter the realm of commercial flights.

Drones come in a variety of sizes, weight and designs. The regulation of drones is also equally diverse. Internationally, whilst the traditional aviation industry has been subject to the framework of an international convention, it is fair to state that no such cohesive international standard or guidelines exist for civil drones. In the European Union, the regulation of unmanned aircraft systems with a maximum take-off mass of less than 150 kg is a matter for individual member states. This has resulted in a lack of consistent and higher standard of regulation across the EU, which has obvious implications for safety and privacy. This is, however, expected to change in the light of the current initiatives for a new regulation that aims to bring all drones, regardless of weight, within the purview of the European Union legal framework.

Law has a difficult job to do in terms of adapting and rising up to ever-changing technologies, without posing a hindrance to innovation and growth. It is imperative that there is a forward-looking, harmonized and appropriate legal framework in place across the European Union in order to support and create a safe, secure and privacy-protected environment for drones to operate. A hallmark of 'good law making' in this respect should be that regulation should not hinder growth and development of the sector by putting European companies at a disadvantage over their (mostly Chinese and US) competitors, but at the same time, it should ensure that the safety and privacy of the operators and the public are protected. It is in this context that this book is highly relevant—not just for policy makers, but also for the producers, operators and users (commercial, civil and casual) of drones regardless of size, weight and configuration.

I have a keen interest in the interaction between law and technology and in particular the challenges the latter raises for the law. I am delighted to have the opportunity to write a Foreword for this book, which considers an area that is very topical but at the same time is in need of more research. In that sense, this book makes a very useful contribution to this field of study. The focus of this book is on professional drones (for, e.g., those used for aerial photography) and commercial drones (for, e.g., those used in precision agriculture, infrastructure inspection and other industrial use), but it also considers casual private use (hobby) to a certain extent. This book starts with an overview of the European Union level policies and regulation that govern civil drones, and the authors argue that the current regulatory framework acts as an impediment for the growth of the drone industry. The authors undertake a useful comparative analysis of the current regulatory framework in Belgium, Spain and the UK, which reveals the adverse impact the lack of harmonization of laws has on the European drone sector as a whole. In the final chapter, the authors endeavour to explore the legal and ethical considerations behind regulation and examine the various regulatory models including self-regulation and co-regulation from a cross-jurisdictional perspective. In particular, they argue that manufacturers of drones should work closely with operators and advocate industry codes of conduct and best practices to ensure the safety, security and privacy of all stakeholders.

As the drone industry takes off further to dizzying heights, it will transform the skies as we see it today. The current legislative initiative at European level to strengthen the regulation of drones will result in one of the significant watershed moments for aviation laws. This book could not be timelier in the light of the ongoing developments in the European Union and beyond.

Abhilash Nair
Senior Lecturer in Internet Law, Aston University, UK
Co-editor, European Journal of Law and Technology

Contents

Abbreviations

AEDRON	Spanish Association of Drones and Similar
AESA	Spanish Safety Aviation Agency
AIP	Aeronautical Information Package
AiRT	Technology Transfer of RPAs for the Creative Industry
ANS	Air Navigation Service
ARPAS-UK	Association of RPAs
ATM	Air Traffic Management
ATO	Approved Training Organization
BCAA	Belgium Civil Aviation Authority
BeUAS	La Fédération Belge de l'Aviation Télépilote
BRLOS	Beyond Direct Radio Line of Sight
BVLOS	Beyond Visual Line of Sight
CAA	Civil Aviation Authority (UK)
CEO	Chief Executive Officer
CIs	Creative Industries
COM SP	Communication Service Provider
CONOPS	Concepts of Operations
CTR	Controlled Traffic Region
D&A	Detect and Avoid System
DGTA	Générale Transport Aérien (Belgium)
DOA	Approved Design Organization
EASA	European Aviation Safety Agency
ENAC	Italian Civil Aviation Authority
ESRG	European RPAS Steering Group
EU	European Union
EVLOS	Extended Visual Line of Sight
FIZ	Flight Information Zone
GCS	Ground Control Station
IAA	Ireland Aviation Authority
ICAO	International Civil Aviation Organization

ICT	Information and Communication Technologies
IFR	Instrument Flight Rule
IPS	Indoor Positioning System
JARUS	Joint Authorities for Regulation of Unmanned Systems
LAPL	Light Aircraft Pilot Licence
MTOW	Maximum Take-Off Weight
NAAs	National Aviation Authorities
NATO	North Atlantic Treaty Organization
NOTAM	Notice to Airmen
OACI	International Civil Aviation Organization
QE	Qualified Entity
RLOS	Direct Radio Line of Sight
RPA	Remotely Piloted Aircraft
RPAS	Remotely Piloted Aircraft System
SARPs	Standards and Recommended Practices
SERA	Standard European Rules of the Air
SMEs	Small- and Medium-Sized Enterprises
SORA	Specific Operational Risk Assessment Specifications
TBD	To Be Determined
TLS	Tolerable Level of Safety
UAS	Unmanned Aerial System
UAV	Unmanned Aerial Vehicle
UCAV	Unmanned Combat Aerial Vehicle
UK	United Kingdom
UPV	Universitat Politècnica de València
USA	The United States of America
VLOS	Visual Line of Sight

Introduction

**Virginia Santamarina Campos, María de Miguel Molina
and Stephan Kröner**

Abstract The aim of this book is to disseminate part of the results of the H2020 European Project AiRT (Technology Transfer of RPAs for the Creative Industry). In particular, we want to present some results to mitigate safety and security concerns when piloting civil drones in the service sector. European policies concerning drones in general are focused on outdoor drone use, but drones can also be employed indoors. Moreover, European countries have fragmented regulations about the use of drones; therefore, European institutions are endeavouring to combine all these regulations. In this sense not only law but also ethics play a key role in providing the industry with guidelines to gain citizens' trust. Therefore, our work is based on four pillars:

1. An analysis of the drone sector in Europe;
2. An in-depth study of the European policies;
3. A comparative analysis of the regulations of some European countries;
4. Primary data from members of the creative industry.

With these results we would like to give advice to the European industry as well as providing new insights for policy makers and the scientific community. The project has received funding from the European Union's Horizon 2020 research and innovation programme under grant agreement no. 732433 (reference: H2020-ICT-2016-2017, www.airt.eu). This book reflects the views of the authors and not necessary the position of the Commission.

1 Scope of the Book

The AiRT project runs from January 2017 to June 2018. The consortium brings together a group of partners from three European countries with a complementary and outstanding range of experiences, skills, competences, and resources.

V. Santamarina Campos (✉) · M. de Miguel Molina · S. Kröner
Universitat Politècnica de València, Valencia, Spain
e-mail: virsanca@upv.es

© The Author(s) 2018
M. de Miguel Molina and V. Santamarina Campos (eds.), *Ethics and Civil Drones*,
SpringerBriefs in Law, https://doi.org/10.1007/978-3-319-71087-7_1

The Universitat Politècnica de València (UPV, Spain) combines experts in creative industries (CIs) on one hand and specialists in robotics and innovative information and communication technology (ICT) solutions on the other hand. From the perspective of specialists in creative activities and aerial filming, Clearhead Media Ltd (UK) has experience in the use of RPASs as a professional filming tool for outdoor purposes. AeroTools UAV-Unmanned Aerial Vehicles (Spain) specializes in developing RPAS systems. It relies on substantial experience in the development of RPAS operation systems, which include advanced functionalities such as automatic obstacle detection, encrypted communication systems, and autonomous RPAS navigation. Pozyx Labs BVBA (Belgium) has developed a novel IPS (indoor positioning system) with which highly precise indoor coordinates can be obtained.

Why is a book on good practices needed?

As will be illustrated very clearly in the second chapter, the drone market presents a real opportunity to foster job creation and a source of innovation and economic growth. For Europe, for instance, about 150,000 jobs are forecast by the AeroSpace and Defence Industries Association of Europe by 2050, excluding employment generated through operator services (European Commission 2014). However, the EU Subcommittee on Civil Use of Drones believes that this approach to estimating job creation through drone operations results in significant underestimations, since it excludes completely new areas of activity that are not necessarily classified as aviation (e.g. surveys, creative industry activities, etc.) (House of Lords 2014). Moreover, the drone industry will not only create new qualified jobs but will foster the emergence of a totally new service industry offering drone operations and aerial work to commercial and state customers. Nevertheless, the legal situation differs in each European country, and technology advances require fast adaption of laws, since special flight environments, like confined spaces, are mostly not considered. These legal uncertainties hinder the exploitation, especially in Europe, of this big and very dynamic market.

Consequently, one focus of this book is the elaboration of a proposal for European legislation for indoor RPAS safety, including both ethical/security and safety risk issues. It will provide recommendations for policies for the European regions and the EU Government, including recommendations to alter the law where necessary and to overcome obstacles (if found) that hinder the use of drones indoors. Although this might seem to be a very challenging task at first glance, when we analysed indoor issues, we reached the conclusion that many of them can be treated in the same way as when operating outdoors. Apart from that, we noticed that, in some European countries, small indoor drones are not considered by any regulation with the exception of professional work.

To which types of drones are the recommendations described in the following chapters of this book addressed?

As will be explained in more detail in the chapter "European Union Policies and Civil Drones", the first rough subdivision/classification of drones can be made according to their mission: military or civilian. The AiRT project has the main goal of providing small and medium-sized creative industries with a drone (more precisely an RPAS—remotely piloted aircraft system) specifically designed for indoor use, which will enable these companies to expand their creativity and offer new and improved services. Thus, in this policy book, we focus on the civilian use of drones for professional and commercial purposes.

As will be discussed in the chapter "The Drone Sector in Europe", the drone market is very large and has tens of applications. As Hassanalian and Abdelkefi (2017) explain, drones can also be classified in the first step according to their flight zone/environment: indoors or outdoors. It has to be kept in mind that the current legislation in the different European countries mainly focuses on the regulation of outdoor use. Here we analyse the current legal state and try to provide some recommendations for proper indoor professional use as well.

Complex matters usually require the cooperation of all the different parties involved, working together in an inter-/transdisciplinary team. Thus, to provide feasible proposals, the AiRT consortium brings together partners from three European countries with complementary experiences, skills, competences, and resources. Therefore, experts in finding ICT solutions for complex topics related to robotics, pioneers in the development of ultra-wideband-based indoor positioning systems for moving objects, drone manufacturers, and specialists in creative activities and aerial filming worked together on the guideline for this good-practice book.

It is important to emphasize that the scenario for which the AiRT project was developed—flying indoors—is not specifically regulated either by the European Aviation Safety Agency (EASA) or by national aviation authorities. As a general rule, these bodies regulate the operation of aircraft only in open airspace, paying no attention to aircraft flying under a ceiling (indoors). This means that a drone operator can fly a drone inside a roofed building with no restriction, and only the permission of the owner is needed. However, this possibility normally fails, since additional issues must be taken into account, such as the civil liability of the operator or the owner in the case of an incident or accident. In other words, since the factual and legal positions are not clarified, the owner or the insurer usually refuses to grant authorization.

The definition of an "indoor space", in terms of regulated operation by civil aviation bodies, is not explicit, but it is generally accepted that indoors means any airspace under a fixed roof or ceiling that could prevent an aircraft from gaining altitude beyond this point. Whether this space has vertical walls or not is irrelevant. In terms of safety, indoor operation offers some positive aspects:

- Short range of flight.
- Always flying with visual line of sight (VLOS), although obstacles can generate shaded areas.
- Short flight time.
- Lack of meteorological variations that might disturb the flight operation.
- Enough resources at hand to provide easy operation (plugs, electrical power, short distances, easy communication, etc.).

On the other hand, violation of privacy, particularly related to private property, such as gathering geographic information (images via satellite, aeroplanes, or drones), has always been an issue for aerial filming. Thus, to maintain high ethical standards, the consideration of ethical research conduct should be part of the project from the very beginning, as ethics are relevant at all stages. In the case of indoor use, it is essential to distinguish between private and public property. In the latter case, the permission of the people affected is a key point. Even in the case of police investigations, the concept of home intromission has been highlighted by the courts. For example, the Spanish Supreme Court (2016), in its Sentence no. 329, 2nd Room, Criminal Court, 20 April 2016, did not accept recorded images made with a drone by the police, as there was no judicial authorization or property permission to film inside that house.

2 Brief Overview of the Different Chapters of the Book

The chapter "The Drone Sector in Europe" illustrates the economic potential of the steadily growing drone market, in Europe as well as China and the US. The latter markets are considered to be the main ones competing with the European one, and, as can be seen in the following chapters, non-uniform European laws may lead to a competitive disadvantage of European companies, in particular SMEs. Therefore, an in-depth analysis of drone applications for professional use by different industries, such as agriculture, media, mining, energy, construction, and so on, has been performed. In addition, special attention has been paid to the creative industry sector, which is particularly affected by the legal confusion. Thus, the importance of a common European framework can be understood, and it is apparent that currently the regulatory barrier seems to be the main impediment to the definitive taking off of the drone industry (Pauner et al. 2015).

In the chapter "European Policies and Civil Drones", the authors analyse the drone policies in the European Union, providing a breakdown of the different types of actors, drones, licenses, and insurance at the European and national levels. Moreover, the ways in which all these policies affect producers and operators are considered. The problems related to licenses, the type of drone and activity, and the opportunity to have insurance can influence the development of the drone industry in the future.

In the chapter "Spain-UK-Belgium Comparative Legal Framework", the different legal frameworks from Spain, the UK, and Belgium are exposed. The CEOs (Chief Executive Officers) of the three companies participating in the project compare their regulations to illustrate the similarities and differences regarding civil drones, not only for outdoor use but also for indoor use. Here the urgency of the pending common European regulatory framework can be seen, and the authors highlight how this could reduce many of the current legal uncertainties.

The chapter "Legal and Ethical Recommendations" is dedicated to legal and above all ethical recommendations. As technology is difficult to regulate, other tools, such as co-regulation and self-regulation, although they can be considered as soft instruments, are useful alternatives for manufacturers and operators of civil drones (Stöcker et al 2017). As part of this project, we organized and held focus groups with drone operators in the three participating countries. Including previous research and the results of these focus group activities, the authors provide recommendations for producers, drone operators, and policy makers. The recommendations cover safety, security, and privacy aspects. Bearing in mind that at present some countries do not regulate the use of drones indoors, drone design by default and professional experience are the most important parameters to guarantee safe and secure drone flights indoors.

References

European Commission (2014) Communication from the Commission to the European Parliament and the Council. A new era for aviation. Opening the aviation market to the civil use of remotely piloted aircraft systems in a safe and sustainable manner. Available via EUR-LEX. http://eur-lex.europa.eu/legal-content/EN/TXT/?uri=CELEX%3A52014DC0207. Accessed 8 September 2017

Hassanalian M, Abdelkefi A (2017) Classifications, applications, and design challenges of drones: a review. Prog in Aerosp Sci 91(May):99–131

House of Lords (2014) EU subcommittee B on civil use of remotely piloted aircraft systems (RPAS). Oral and written evidence. Available via Parliament. http://www.parliament.uk/civil-rpas. Accessed 8 September 2017

Pauner C, Kamara I, Viguri J (2015) Drones. Current challenges and standardisation solutions in the field of privacy and data protection. ITU Kaleidosc: trust in the information society (K-2015), pp 1–7

Spanish Supreme Court (2016) Sentence no. 329, 2nd room, criminal court. Available via vLEX. https://supremo.vlex.es/vid/637465649#section_6. Accessed 18 August 2017

Stöcker C, Bennett R, Nex F, Gerke M, Zevenbergen J (2017) Review of the current state of UAV regulations. Remote Sens 9(5):459–485

The Drone Sector in Europe

Blanca de Miguel Molina and Marival Segarra Oña

Abstract The aim of this chapter is to review the industry sector in Europe, which involves big companies as well as SMEs. The leading European countries, the main competitors, and the main competitive advantages of the industry are analysed. We have identified five different segments in which companies compete based on distinctive features (toys, hobby/leisure, professional, commercial, and military). The homogenization of the industry, especially in the toy, hobby, and commercial subsectors, is mainly led by big companies, which at the same time also represent the largest market share. We have concluded that there are no entry barriers besides technology and commercial distribution, but the main difficulty that is hampering the industry's expansion is regulation. This affects in particular the hobby/leisure and commercial drone segments, some areas more than others; while agricultural and military drones are expanding and evolving rapidly, professional filming and photography and toys are still too dependent on safety or legal issues, such as privacy concerns. It is also remarkable that companies from China and the USA are reaching the top positions. This should be taken into consideration by European policy makers, as the decisions made in the next years will be the key to the development of the sector in Europe.

1 Introduction

Why is it important to analyse the drone market first? There are two main reasons. Firstly, it illustrates the potential of this steadily growing market, which, due to the lack of unification of national laws in a common European regulation, is not fully exploited. Secondly, it shows why it is so difficult to reach a common agreement:

B. de Miguel Molina (✉) · M. Segarra Oña
Department of Management, Universitat Politècnica de València, Valencia, Spain
e-mail: bdemigu@omp.upv.es

© The Author(s) 2018
M. de Miguel Molina and V. Santamarina Campos (eds.), *Ethics and Civil Drones*,
SpringerBriefs in Law, https://doi.org/10.1007/978-3-319-71087-7_2

tens of drone application and thus drone characteristics (e.g., size, weight, engine power, range of the aircraft, etc.) exist. Thus, before regulating markets (drones), first the market has to be described and analysed in detail to find a proper solution that pleases all: industry, governments, the military, researchers, and the general public.

How can we define the drone industry? This question needs to be answered to structure the information, since up to now information regarding drones has not been easy to find. This might be because the regulations do not fully support their use, because military uses are still the most common ones and the army industry treats everything as strictly secret, because technology is developing so fast that sharing information would help competitors, or because the rise of the industry is so fast that there is no time to analyse data and research the insights or to disseminate news.

Although difficulties exist, we will retrieve information regarding the drone industry and restructure it to try to provide readers with an engaging chapter that helps them to understand the main facts, characteristics, and strategic opportunities that the industry currently offers.

The Cambridge English Dictionary offers two definitions of a drone:

- an aircraft that does not have a pilot but is controlled by someone on the ground and is used especially for dropping bombs or for surveillance (meaning careful watching of a place);
- an aircraft without a pilot that is controlled by someone on the ground and is used especially as a hobby.

These definitions are very useful, as they clarify not only the meaning but also the main uses of drones. In the second definition, we could include different uses that have recently appeared, such as safety purposes, transport and delivery, and so on. As there is no unique word to name an aircraft without a pilot, it is also quite usual to find the following definitions:

UAV (*Unmanned Aerial Vehicle*)
UAS (*Unmanned Aerial System*)
UCAV (*Unmanned Combat Aerial Vehicle*)
RPA (*Remotely Piloted Aircraft*)
RPAS (*Remotely Piloted Aircraft System*).

Drone and UAV/UAS are commonly used to refer to military uses and RPA/RPAS to name drones with civilian purposes.

Although drones seem to be a very modern invention and there is no consensus regarding the first use of a drone, it seems that drones started to be used for military purposes. The first patent for a "Method of and apparatus for controlling mechanism of moving vessels or vehicles" was filed by Nikola Tesla in 1898 (Infographic 2016), although it was in 1951 that the first prototypes of Ryan's Q-2C Firebee pilotless aircraft were tested. Designed by the company Ryan Aeronautical as a target contract from the North American Air Force, this drone was in production for over 40 years and is still being used by some military organizations (San Diego Air and Space Museum 2017).

Nowadays, different patents are being filed that are as specific as drones without propellers (application number KR20150177849 20151214) or drones capable of operating in an aqueous environment (application number US201614994662 20160113), showing how interesting the industry can be for new companies and new business ideas.

2 Overview of the Drone Sector

The use of drones has been growing during the last years, and the two main market segments (military and hobby/leisure) have turned into three, depending on their final uses: military, commercial, and hobby. Figure 1 presents the estimated evolution of the three segments. Although the military segment is the main market by value, the figure indicates that the other two segments will expand during the next years.

Although the use of drones has generated considerable controversy due to privacy and safety awareness, nowadays people's perceptions about "good" uses of drones related to civil uses (commercial and hobby) have changed their image and acceptance (Table 1). Among the accepted uses of unmanned aerial vehicles, we may cite those related to health (transport of blood and defibrillators), humanitarian

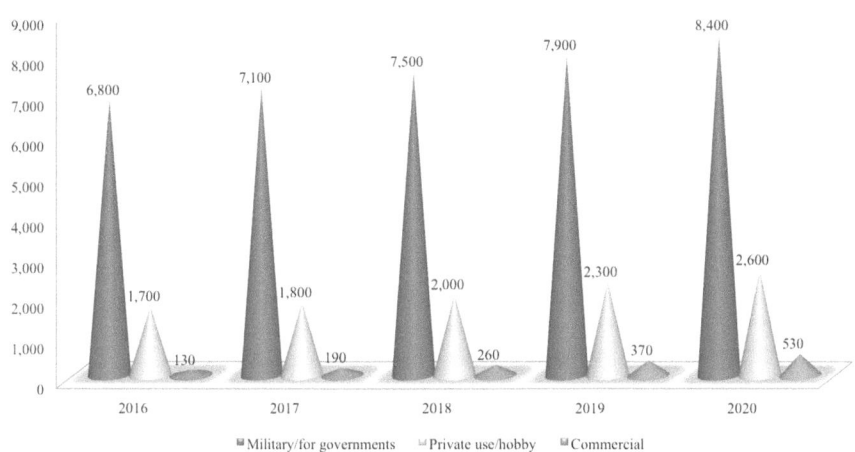

Fig. 1 Estimated value of drone market segments worldwide, 2016–2010 (mill. US$). *Source* Own elaboration from data of Moe et al. (2016)

Table 1 Acceptable drone applications

Accepted uses	
Source	Use
Amukele et al. (2017)	Blood transportation
Hardy et al. (2017)	Mapping malaria vector habitats
Pulver et al. (2016)	Transporting automated external defibrillators
Chabot and Francis (2016)	Bird detection
Hodgson et al. (2017)	Surveying marine fauna
Sankey et al. (2017)	Forest monitoring
Casella et al. (2017)	Mapping coral reefs
Szantol et al. (2017)	Mapping orangutan habitat
Chowdhury et al. (2017)	Disaster response and relief
Restas (2015)	Supporting disaster management (earthquakes, floods, fires)

Source Own elaboration from different sources

actions (drones for social goods and humanitarian purposes), shipping products to customers (Amazon's fleet of drones), or ecological applications (surveying fauna and forest monitoring), among others.

However, not only are the applications of drones evolving; the expected revenue increase in the next 10 years is also impressive. According to Tractica (2017c), the greatest evolution will take place in North America, Asia, and Europe, which are also the areas of the market leaders nowadays.

The industry is growing fast, driven mainly by technology. The number of drone-specific exhibitions and conferences is rising (for instance UAV Expo in Brussels or AUVSI's Xponential in the USA), and rapid industry developments are evident. Some examples are drones with robotic arms that can grab objects and magnetic pieces containing drone engines that can be adjusted to objects and turn them into drones (prototypes by Prodrone, a Japanese company). Additionally, though, safety and research are leading the change, and interesting conclusions are being drawn; indeed, the British company Consortiq's CQNet, by collecting and analysing data, defines landing with minimal battery charge as the main reason for the lack of drone safety. The possibilities of the industry are immense, and currently the regulatory barrier (Pauner et al. 2015) seems to be the main impediment to the drone industry taking off definitively (Fig. 2).

Regarding manufacturers, China's DJI followed by the French Parrot occupy the top positions, according to Droneii (2016a), followed by Chinese and North American companies, as reflected in Fig. 3.

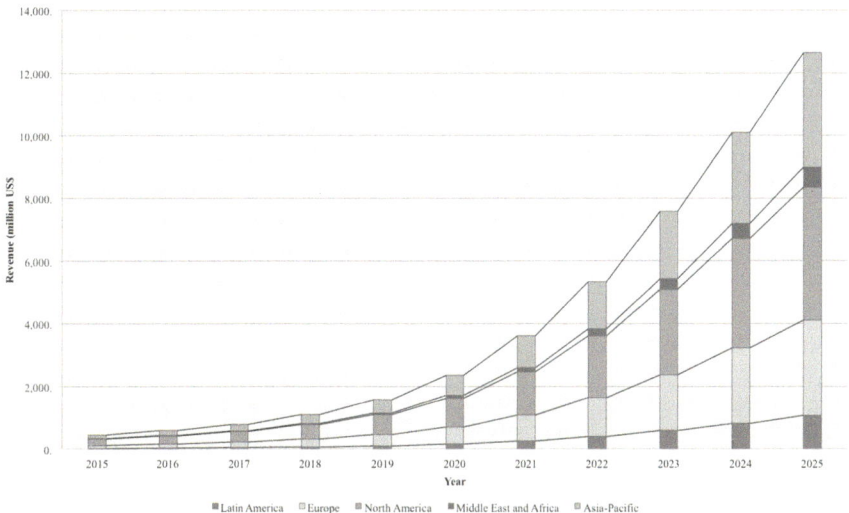

Fig. 2 Projected commercial drone revenue from 2015 to 2025 (in million US dollars). *Source* Own elaboration from data of Tractica (2017c)

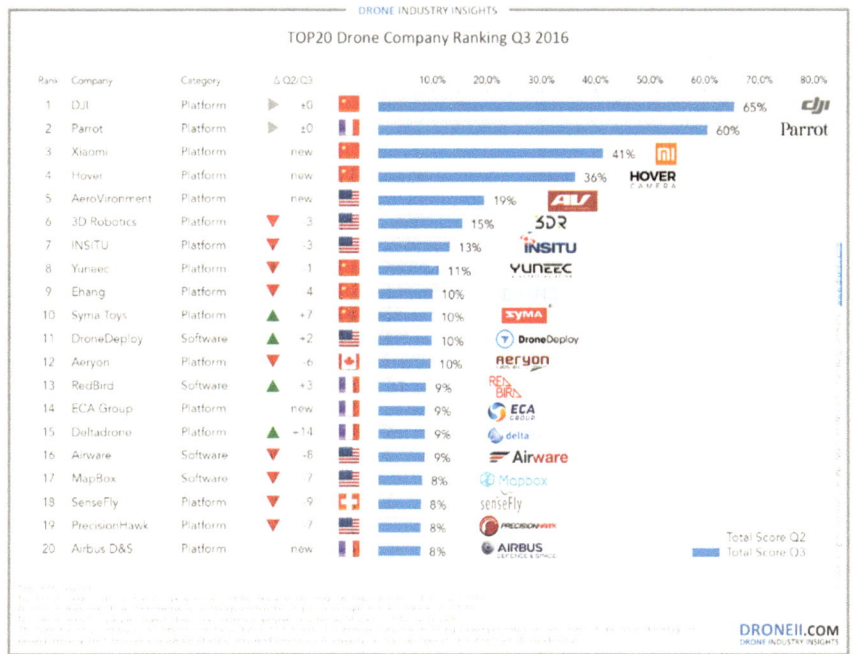

Fig. 3 Drone company ranking, Q3 2016 (Droneii 2016a), with permission of the company (https://www.droneii.com/top20-drone-company-ranking-q3-2016)

3   Market Segments

Segmentation is a market strategy focused on the consumer side, which allows a better fit between products and users' requirements (Smith 1956). A firm that follows a market segmentation strategy is expected to increase its profitability (Wind 1978), although an empirical study is needed. In this study the basic demographic data, such as customer characteristics, users' needs, final use, and so on, are necessary to determine the different existing segments. This goal of this study is to identify and classify the market segments or "sets of buyers" that indeed will be the industry's target groups and will define companies' marketing strategies (Venter et al. 2015).

Markets for drones tend to be segmented in relation to their use, which also corresponds to price ranges. Generally, the sector is structured in three groups: military, commercial, and hobby. For our analysis, however, we have divided the market into five groups (Table 2), which we have defined after taking into consideration the theoretical market segmentation background.

Forecasting undertaken for the industry by the Teal Group (2013) and Tractica (2016, 2017a), among others, predicts future growth for all the market segments. For example, concerning the hobby segment, Tractica (2016) indicates that the revenue worldwide amounted to US\$1865.65 million in the year 2015. Moreover, it estimates that the revenue for this segment will be US\$3528.73 million in 2018 and US\$5031.36 million in 2022. In relation to the military segment, the Teal Group (2013) estimates that the production value worldwide will be US\$2629.1 million in 2015, while it will be US\$4075.4 million in 2018 and US\$8076.4 million in 2022.

Table 2 Market segments for drones

Use	Customer target	Price (€)	Example of drones
Group 1—Toys	Children	49.95	X_DRONE_ATOM_221
Group 2—Hobby	Young people and adults	179.99	Cheerson CX 20
Group 3—Professional	Professionals (for aerial filming and photography services)	4875 549	DJI Inspire 1 Pro Parrot BEBOP 2 FPV
Group 4—Commercial	Companies in industries such as agriculture, media, mining, energy, construction, etc.	19,921.2 10,172.5	Altura Zenith (Aerialtronics) Alta 6 (Freefly)
Group 5—Military	Governments	Not available	RQ-2A Pioneer

Sources Teal Group (2013), Tractica (2016, 2017a), and own elaboration through an analysis of the companies in the sector

The use of drones for commercial purposes in outdoor environments has increased in recent years, and this tendency will continue in the future. Their use for commercial purposes means their use in sectors such as infrastructure, transport, insurance, media and entertainment, telecommunications, agriculture, security, and mining (PwC 2016). Tractica (2017c) indicates that the worldwide revenue for commercial drones was US$452.43 million in the year 2015. It estimates that the revenue will be US$1110.59 million in 2018 and US$5334.68 million in 2022.

Figure 4 shows that the highest estimated growth in the next years will occur in the commercial segment; that is, companies in other industries will demand more drones for monitoring activities, mapping, and surveying (Narkus-Kramer 2017). In the future more industries will probably find new applications for drones that the current technology does not allow; then drone manufacturers will offer these features in their products (Ott 2012). Movement to the commercial segments can be detected nowadays in companies such as DJI, which has started to partner with other companies to offer drones with software specializing in agriculture, mining, and construction.

Focusing on the European market, Table 3 might explain why companies are interested in the drone industry and are developing specific software for drones. The turnover data show that the highest values are for energy, construction, agriculture, real estate, and transport. However, if we consider turnover by firm, interesting markets for drone manufacturers will be energy, water and waste, postal and courier activities, telecommunication, and mining. All these sectors are currently target markets for drone manufacturers.

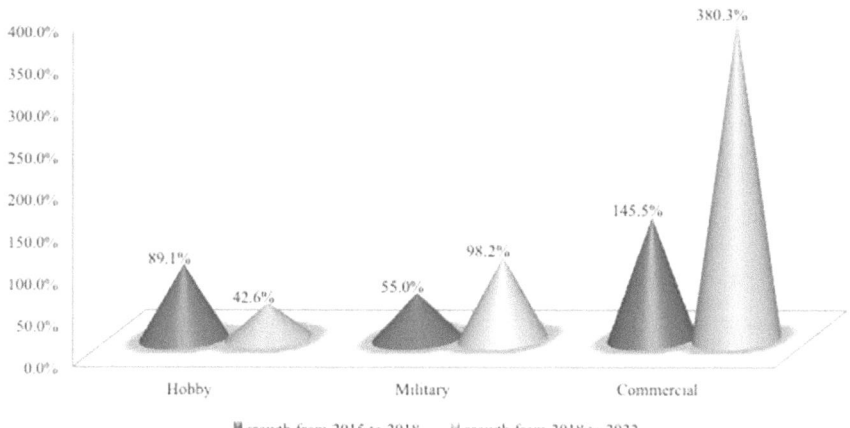

Fig. 4 Estimated growth for segments in the next years. *Source* Own elaboration from data of the Teal Group (2013) and Tractica (2016, 2017c)

Table 3 European data related to industries in which outdoor drones can be used (EU 20 countries 2014)

Sector	Number of firms	Turnover[a]	Largest number of firms	Largest turnover
Electricity, gas, steam, and air conditioning supply	87,465	1,478,875.8	France, Spain, Italy, Czech Republic	Germany, Italy, United Kingdom, France
Water supply; sewerage, waste management, and remediation activities	75,738	253,000.0	France, Italy, Poland	Germany, United Kingdom, France, Italy
Construction	3,441,304	1,577,430.1	France, Italy, Spain, Germany, United Kingdom	France, United Kingdom, Germany, Italy
Land transport and transport via pipelines	916,520	530,000.0	Spain, Poland, Italy, France	Germany, France, United Kingdom, Italy
Postal and courier activities	65,800	110,000.0	United Kingdom, Germany, Netherlands, Spain	Germany, United Kingdom, France
Insurance	n.a.	n.a.	Germany, France, Spain	Germany, France, Italy
Motion picture, video, and TV programme production; sound recording and music publishing activities	138,246	70,573.2	France, United Kingdom, Netherlands, Sweden, Germany	United Kingdom, France, Germany
Advertising and market research	300,440	160,000.0	Netherlands, Germany, France, Spain	United Kingdom, Germany, France
Telecommunication	45,377	378,000.0	United Kingdom, Poland, France, Spain, Italy	United Kingdom, France, Germany
Agriculture	178,126.54[b]	418,713.55[c]	France, Spain, United Kingdom, Germany	France, Germany, Italy, Spain, United Kingdom

(continued)

Table 3 (continued)

Sector	Number of firms	Turnover[a]	Largest number of firms	Largest turnover
Security and investigation activities	56,000	46,000.0	France, United Kingdom, Hungary, Germany	United Kingdom, France, Germany
Mining and quarrying	19,237	223,983.5	Italy, Germany, Spain, France, Poland, Romania, Portugal	Norway, Italy, United Kingdom, Netherlands
Architectural and engineering activities; technical testing and analysis	1,005,668	329,000.0	Italy, Germany, France, Spain, United Kingdom	United Kingdom, Germany, France
Real estate activities	1,369,456	484,231.4	Germany, Italy, France, Spain	Germany, France, United Kingdom

Source Eurostat
[a]Millions €
[b]Utilized agricultural area (thousands of hectares)
[c]Output of the agricultural industry at basic prices (after taxes but including subsidies; million €)

4   Main Competitors in the Sector

Competitors in the drone sector operate globally, and this environment increases the rivalry in the market. To obtain a list of competitors in the industry, we used different lists obtained from sources specialized in the field (PwC 2016; Droneii 2016a) and a statistical database (Statista).

Through the analysis of the information on the web pages of the companies in these lists, including the products offered by the companies and their prices, we have organized the competitors using the same groups of markets as defined in Sect. 2. Therefore, we have established five groups of competitors depending on the market segment in which they sell their products (Tables 4, 5, 6, 7, 8):

- Group 1: manufacturers offering drones to consumer markets as toys,
- Group 2: manufacturers offering drones to consumer markets as hobby products,
- Group 3: manufacturers offering drones for professional purposes,
- Group 4: manufacturers offering drones for specific industries,
- Group 5: manufacturers offering military drones.

Table 4 Manufacturers and their products in Group 1 (Toys)

Company	Country	Drone models	Prices (€)	Sells through own website	Sells through Amazon	Sells through others (e.g.)	Support
Parrot	France	Minidrones (different names)	100–130	Yes	Yes	www.droneprix.es	Email, phone
		AR Drone	180				
Extreme Flyers	UK	Micro Drone 3.0	172	Yes	Not available	No	Community
Syma Toys	China	X8 (different models)	150	No	Yes	aliexpress.com tomtop.com	Email, phone
Cheerson	China	Different models	42–110	Yes	Yes	aliexpress.com tomtop.com	Email, website
UDI RC	China	Different models	50–160	No	Yes	tomtop.com	Email, phone
Drone WL Toys	Netherlands	Different models	50–280	Yes	Yes	aliexpress.com tomtop.com	Email, website

Source Manufacturers' web pages; Amazon, aliexpress.com, tomtop.com, etc.

Table 5 Manufacturers and their products in Group 2 (Hobby)

Company	Country	Drone models	Prices (€)	Sells through own website	Sells through Amazon	Sells through others (e.g.)	Support
3D Robotics	USA	Solo with camera GoPro	653	Yes	Yes	www.BestBuy.com	Email
AEE technology	China	Toruk AP 10 Pro	254	Yes	Yes	www.andorrafreemarket.com	Email
		Toruk AP 11	593			www.andorrafreemarket.com	
		Condor Elite	1300	New	No	www.artencraft.be	
		Condor advanced		New	No	Displayed at www.aeeusa.com	
Cheerson	China	CX	297–424	Yes	Yes	www.tomtop.es	Email, website
DJI	China	Spark	424–593	Yes	Yes	http://www.bestbuy.com	Email, online, phone, forum
		Phantom 4	1272			www.tomtop.es	
		Mavic	848–1102			www.tomtop.es	
		Flame Wheel	203–254			www.HobbyReal.com	
EHang	China	Ghostdrone 2.0	540–990	No	Yes	www.tomtop.com	Phone, email, community
Fleye	Belgium	Fleye Racer	590	Yes	No	No	Email
		Fleye Helmet	290				
		Fleye Dudted	1180				

(continued)

Table 5 (continued)

Company	Country	Drone models	Prices (€)	Sells through own website	Sells through Amazon	Sells through others (e.g.)	Support
GoPro	USA	Karma	1000–1400	Yes	Yes	www.todrone.com	Phone, chat
Helico aerospace/ AirDog	Latvia	AirDog	1356	No	Yes	No	Email, community
Hover	China	Hover Camera	424	No	No	www.apple.com	Email
Hubsan	China	H109S X4 Pro	339–678	No	Yes	www.gearbest.com	Email, phone
Krossblade Aerosp.	USA	SkyProwler	2204	Yes	No	No	Website
Onago fly	USA	1 Plus	254	No	Yes	www.gearbest.com	Email, phone
Parrot	France	Bebop	500–700	Yes	Yes	www.bestbuy.com	Email, phone
		Disco	900–1000			www.apple.com	
Squadrone system	USA	Hexo+	1000	Yes	Yes	www.adorama.com	Email, website
SwellPro	Germany	Splash Drone Fisherman	1187	Yes	Yes	www.urbandrones.com	Email, phone
Walkera technology Co	China	AIBAO	398	Yes	Yes	www.tomtop.com	Email, phone
		VITUS	678			www.HobbyReal.com	
		Scout X4	€1150			www.HobbyReal.com	
		Tali H500	€1400			http://www.dx.com	
		Different models for racing drones	136–381			www.rcmoment.com	

(continued)

Table 5 (continued)

Company	Country	Drone models	Prices (€)	Sells through own website	Sells through Amazon	Sells through others (e.g.)	Support
Xiaomi	China	Mi Drone	487	No	Yes	www.tomtop.com	Email, phone
Yuneec	China	Breeze	339	No	Yes	www.fnac.es	Email, phone
		Typhoon	678–1272			www.bestbuy.com	
Zerotech	China	Dobby	339	No	Yes	www.tomtop.com	Email

Source manufacturers' web pages; Amazon, aliexpress.com, Apple store, etc.

Table 6 Manufacturers and their products in Group 3 (Professional)

Company	Country	Drone models	Prices (€)	Sells through own website	Sells through Amazon	Sells through others (e.g.)	Support
3D Robotics	USA	Solo with camera Sony	4239	Yes	Yes	www.onedrone.com	Email
DJI	China	Inspire 2	2543–5256	Yes	Yes	www.onedrone.com	Email, online, phone, forum
		Matrice	2797–4239				
		Spreading Wings	1017–1272				
Aeronavics	New Zealand	SkyJib	1865–2119	No	No	www.aerogenix.com	Email, phone
Cyphy	USA	PARC	4239	No	No	No	Email
Ascending technologies	Germany	Astec Firefly	2543	No	No	No	Phone and email
		Astec Hummingbird	3391				
		Astec Pelican	4239				
Walkera technology	China	Voyager 4	3190	Yes	Yes	www.aliexpress.com	Email, phone
		QR X900	3730		No	www.hobbyreal.com	
Zerotech	China	Highone Pro	6104	No	No	http://www.rchobby-avenues.co.uk	Email
SwellPro	Germany	Splash Drone Auto	6104	Yes	No	www.urbandrones.com	Email, phone
Xaircraft	China	Xplanet	4239	No	No	www.aliexpress.com	Email
		Xmission	4400			www.dronedron.com	

(continued)

Table 6 (continued)

Company	Country	Drone models	Prices (€)	Sells through own website	Sells through Amazon	Sells through others (e.g.)	Support
Yuneec	China	Typhoon H520	2119–3815	No	New	www.futurdrone.com	Email, phone
		Tornado H920 Plus	2713		Yes	www.futurdrone.com	
Microdrones	Germany	MD4-200	1695	No	No	No	Customer portal, phone, email
Ascending technologies	Germany	Astec Firefly	2543	No	No	No	Phone, email
		Astec Hummingbird	3391				
		Astec Pelican	4239				

Source manufacturers' web pages, Amazon, and searches through google.com

Table 7 Manufacturers and their products in Group 4 (Commercial)

Company	Country	Drone models	Prices (€)	Sells through own website	Sells through Amazon	Sells through others	Support
3D Robotics	USA	Site Scan (includes drone Solo)	10,173	Yes	Yes	No	Email
Aerialtronics	Netherlands	Altura Zenith (platform)	19,921	No	Yes	www. easyshopdrone.com	Email
Aeryon	Canada	SkyRanger	169,542	No	No	Worldwide distribution channel	Website, phone
DJI	China	Agras	13,563	No	No	Worldwide distribution channel	Email, online, phone, forum
Freefly	USA	Alta 6	10,173	Yes	Yes	http://www. quadrocopter.com	Forum, website
		Alta 8	14,835			http://www. quadrocopter.com	
INSITU	USA	Scan Eagle	84,771	No	No	No	Phone, email
Intuitive aerial	Sweden	Aerigon MKII	34,756	No	No	No	Phone, client portal
Kespry	USA	Kespry drone system	25,431 (yearly lease)	No	No	No	Email, web
Aeronavics	New Zealand	SkyJib (with RED camera)	12,716	No	No	www.1uas.com/	Email, phone
AeroVironments	USA	Quantix	12,716–25,431	No	No	No	Email, phone
Delair-Tech	France	UX5	43,233	No	No	Worldwide distribution channel	Email, phone
		DT18	31,959			Worldwide distribution channel	
		DT26X	102,861			Worldwide distribution channel	

(continued)

Table 7 (continued)

Company	Country	Drone models	Prices (€)	Sells through own website	Sells through Amazon	Sells through others	Support
Kespry	USA	Kespry drone system	25,431 (yearly lease)	No	No	No	Email, web
Parrot	France	Ebee SQ	11,400–12,600	Yes	No	www.tecnitop.com	Email, phone
Precision Hawk	USA	Lancaster 5	10,935	Yes	No	No	Phone, web
Sensefly (Parrot)	Switzerland	eBee	25,000	No	No	Worldwide distribution channel	Email, phone, customer portal
		Albris	14,411			Worldwide distribution channel	
Zerotech	China	E-Pic	12,521–15,259	No	No	www.skytechs.com	Email
Microdrones	Germany	MD4-1000	25,431	No	No	Worldwide distribution channel	Customer portal, phone, email
		MD4-3000	44,081			Worldwide distribution channel	
Ascending technologies	Germany	Astec Falcon 8	26,279	No	No	Worldwide distribution channel	Phone, email
Action Drones	USA	AD2	5680	No	No	www. spacecitydrones.com	Phone, email

Source manufacturers' web pages and searches through google.com

Group 1 (Toys) includes manufacturers of drones of which the customer target is children, who will have their first experience of flying drones. Table 4 presents some examples of the companies included in this group, indicating that the prices are around €100 and that some models carry a camera while others do not. Companies use external selling channels, such as Amazon, to reach their customers. European manufacturers in this group have to compete with Chinese firms.

Group 2 (Hobby) involves manufacturers of products that are focused on different customers from Group 1, who want to film themselves and their relatives and/ or friends while participating in action sports or other activities. Taking into account the higher purchase capacity of customers in this group, drones will include more technical features than those in Group 1. These features might include a camera and storage function (e.g. Micro-SD card or similar). These recreational customers are also looking for customizable and programmable features, ease of use, durability, and flight time. They are willing to pay between €500 and €1500 for drones included in Group 2, and they buy them directly from the manufacturer's website, through Amazon, and through other dealers, such as www.aliexpress.com or www. tomtop.com (Table 5). This group seems to be more profitable considering the number of companies involved in it. However, companies have to compete with an important rival, the Chinese firm DJI.

Group 3 (Professional) includes manufacturers of drones for professional filming and photography. Drone operators whose main activity is aerial filming services use these types of products, which are sometimes high models of those shown in Group 2. The prices are below €10,000, and DJI is an important rival. This company is very active in partnering with other firms for both hardware and software. Nowadays, DJI competes with firms that offer drones with cameras (Inspire 2, Phantom 4 Pro) and with those that offer drone platforms to carry different cameras (Matrice 600 Pro, Spreading Wings S1000 +). It is difficult for smaller companies to offer both products, so they need to choose between them. Offering a platform without a camera would allow customers to fit the drone with professional cameras, such as RED and Alexa, with a higher final cost for the user. These cameras are heavy and need bigger drones with the capacity to fly with a heavy camera.

Group 4 (Commercial) involves manufacturers that develop solutions for specific industries. The value of the offering is based more on the software and applications than on the drone itself. Companies partner (Droneii 2016b) with software firms (Airmap, Facebook), hardware firms (Intel, Leica Geosystems), and cameras makers (Sony) in an effort to increase the value associated with their products. As a result, the final price of the solution, which includes a drone, is higher. Moreover, some drone manufacturers offer the software with a yearly fee license (Kespry), following the rules from the software industry. Group 4 also includes companies that offer services through a drone instead of selling it. The company designs and assembles the drone, but its business model is built on offering services related to drones as its value proposition. Therefore, Group 4 includes companies offering only the product (drone and software), the product and services, and only services.

Table 8 Manufacturers and their products in Group 5 (Military)

Company	Country	Drone models	Prices (€)	Sells through own website	Sells through Amazon	Sells through others	Support
AeroVironments	USA	Different models (RAVEN, PUMA, WASP)	n.a.	No	No	No	Email, phone
Aeryon	Canada	SkyRanger	169,542	No	No	No	Website, phone
Airbus D&S	France	Different models	n.a.	No	No	No	Phone
INSITU (Boeing)	USA	Scan Eagle	84,771	No	No	No	Phone, website
		Integrator	n.a.				
		RQ-21A Blackjack	n.a.				
General Atomics	USA	Predator	17 mill	No	No	No	Phone
		Reaper	48 mill				
FLIR	Norway	Black Hornet Nano	25,431–42,386	No	No	No	Phone, email
Thales	France	Different models and sizes	n.a.	No	No	No	Customer service platform
IAI	Israel	Different models	n.a.	No	No	No	Phone, email, cell
EMT	Germany	Luna and others	n.a.	No	No	No	Email, phone, website
Northrop Grumman	USA	Global Hawk	n.a.	No	No	No	Phone
UAV Solutions	USA	Phoenix models	n.a.	Yes	No	Yes	Website, phone, email

Source manufacturers' web pages and searches through google.com

Few companies in Group 4 sell through their own online shop. Table 7 indicates that these companies are the ones with lower prices. The rest of the firms tend to sell directly to customers or use specialized dealers.

Group 5 (Military) includes manufacturers focused on defence and military purposes. They sell to armies, governments, and defence organizations like NATO (North Atlantic Treaty Organization). Companies need to fulfil the requirements specified by each government in security assurance relations. Some companies have started to offer products to customers in Group 4, as some of their products can be used for surveillance and monitoring. This might indicate their interest in the increase in the commercial market and the capacity of some of these industries to assume higher costs in buying drones and the services associated with them. Military companies have skilled resources and technologies that can be used for different purposes.

The software incorporated into drones has been demonstrated to be an importance source of value creation. This has produced parallel growth in companies focused on software development. Among these companies are Airware (USA), Dedrone (Germany), DroneDeploy (USA), MapBox (USA), PIX4D (Switzerland), RedBird (France), SkyWards (USA), and Skyworks Aerial System (USA). Most companies are from the United States and others are from European countries, outlining the drone industry. Some solutions allow the processing and analysis of data from images captured through drones, adapting their solutions to different industries (mining, agriculture, surveying, construction, etc.). Other companies work as developers of drone detection (Dedrone), flying simulators (Redbird), and platforms that publish data obtained through other drone software (MapBox).

The main conclusions that we could obtain from the analysis of the competitors are the following:

(a) As shown by the number of companies that enter the drone market every year, there are no high barriers to entry.

(b) Companies have started to extend their customer segments, especially the biggest companies in the sector. This can be observed in DJI, 3D Robotics, and Parrot, but also in some companies operating in both the commercial and the military segment.

(c) Camera makers and software developers are strategic partners for drone companies. For example, big companies use cameras and software to offer products with a higher value and adapt them to each segment. The final cost of the solutions will increase with these additional features. Increasingly these customers pay for the software included as an annual fee.

(d) New features spread rapidly through the industry (incremental innovations such as extended flight time, better cameras, less noise, auto charging batteries, etc.).

(e) The high number of competitors in the market might explain why they offer more than one selling channel for their products, although this is less usual for higher-priced drones (the military segment and some commercial solutions).

(f) While companies are selling lower-priced drones online, higher-priced drones are usually sold directly after contact by email or through a worldwide distribution channel.

(g) The main support is obtained by users through channels including phone, email, and web pages.

(h) The price of military drones is not readily available and might depend strongly on the amount ordered, extra features, and the strategic point of view.

5 Main European Figures

Tractica's (2017b) data indicate that the revenue from commercial drones in Europe in 2015 was US$99.53 million. Moreover, they estimate important growth in revenue from 2016 to 2025. They forecast US$250.99 million in revenues for 2018, US$1248.32 million for 2022, and US$3035.33 million for 2025. Figure 5 presents these data in percentages, showing the highest growth period as 2018–2022. In terms of units, the current use of drones in Europe (SESAR 2016) is limited to around 1000 military drones, 1–1.5 million consumer drones, and 10,000 units of commercial drones. SESAR (2016) forecasts 200,000 units in 2025 and 395,000 in 2035 for the commercial domain, agriculture being the main domain with 150,000 units in 2035. Other important domains are energy (10,000 units), public safety and security (60,000), e-commerce and delivery (70,000), mobility and transport (1000), and others (media, mining and construction, insurance, real estate, telecommunication, and academic research) with 100,000 units in 2035. On the other hand, the main opportunities in the sector will be associated with service activities (related to software, data, and flying operations), which will absorb 80% of the total economic impact in 2035 (SESAR 2016).

Table 9 shows the location of drone companies in Europe and indicates that the main countries are the United Kingdom, Italy, Germany, and France. The importance of these countries is also clear when data about international trade and the number of operators registered are exposed. International trade data indicate that the country that imports the most drones is the United Kingdom, followed by India, Italy, Azerbaijan, Germany, Turkey, France, Singapore, and Brazil (The Guardian 2015a). On the other hand, the main exporting countries of drones are Israel, the United States, Canada, Russia, France, Austria, Italy, Germany, and China (The Guardian 2015b). Other sources include Spain and Switzerland among the important countries in the European drone market (Wichmann 2017). Tables 4, 5, 6, 7, 8 present the European manufacturers in each of the five segments analysed, and they included some of these countries. The leading European (Government Office for Science 2017) RPAS manufacturers are Parrot (France), AirRobot (Germany), Ascending Technologies (Germany), MicroDrones (Germany), UAV Factory (Latvia), and Aerialtronics (Netherlands).

Data about the number of drone operators certified are published by the aviation authorities of each country, although these data are not always available, because in

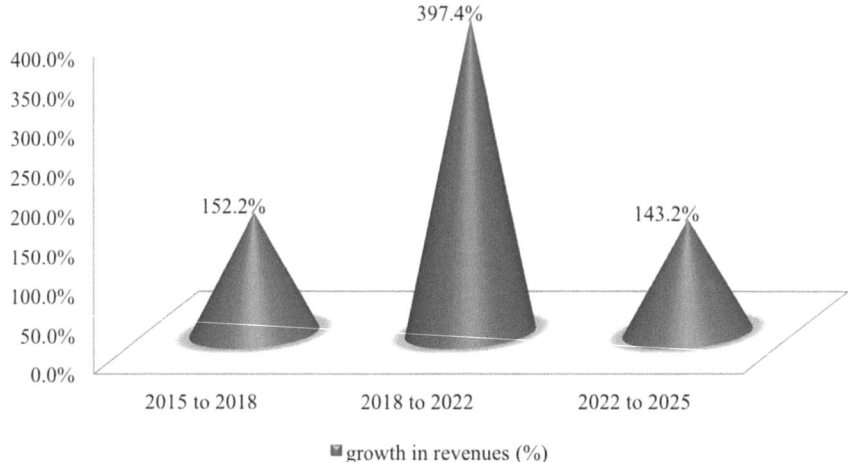

Fig. 5 Estimated growth in revenues for commercial drones in Europe. *Source* Own elaboration from data of Tractica (2017b)

Table 9 Drone manufacturers by European country in relation to important manufacturers' countries

Country	Number of manufacturers	Country	Number of manufacturers
USA	229	Israel, Spain	16
China	38	Australia	15
UK	34	Austria, Netherlands, Sweden, Switzerland	8
Italy	31	Portugal, Romania, Slovenia, Ukraine	4
Germany	30	Belarus, Belgium, Bulgaria, Czech Republic, Finland, Serbia	3
France	28	Estonia, Hungary, Latvia	2
Canada, Russia	20	Denmark, Greece, Ireland, Luxembourg	1

Source AUVSI (2016)

some countries, such as Germany, there is no registration of drone operators. Table 10 presents the number of licensed operators for some countries. This number has increased in the last years and is continuing to grow, indicating the attraction to this market of new professionals and companies. The activities carried out by these professionals and companies differ by country. For example, in Spain (Todrone 2016) the main activities using drones undertaken by companies and RPAS operators are audiovisual/leisure (45.8%), infrastructure/mining (16.9%), and agriculture/environment (14.5%). In the United Kingdom (Government Office for Science 2017), however, the main activities are aerial photography/video, surveying/mapping, aerial cinematography, and industrial inspection.

Table 10 Certified drone operators by country

Country	Operators	Source
United Kingdom	3046	Civil Aviation Authority (2017)
Ireland	172	IAA (2017)
France	2250	Statista (2016)
Spain	2420	AESA (2017)
Italy	972	ENAC (2017)
Germany	n.a.	n.a.
Switzerland	n.a.	n.a.
Belgium	152	www.beuas.be/fr/membership/licentie

Source different sources (n.a.: not available)

6 Conclusions

In this chapter the available information regarding the drone industry has been compiled and analysed. Despite the sector having both technological and economic importance, there are important barriers preventing its expansion. The biggest barrier to the industry's development is regulation, which limits the use of drones based mainly on two different reasons: safety and security/privacy. Europe has to resolve this issue as quickly as possible, before the other two big economic countries, the USA and China, achieve advances that are too great compared with those of European firms, leading to an increased gap in academic, technological, business, and social development areas.

Although the first drones were produced in 1951 and the first document regarding unpiloted aircraft was patented in 1898, the main evolution of the drone industry has occurred in recent years, led mainly by military needs. Nowadays the most innovative drone uses can be associated with collaboration (health and drugs delivery, emergency surveillance, security, etc.) and commercial efficiency (agriculture, topography, etc.).

It is important to distinguish among the different segments within the drone industry, since the needs and characteristics of different end users are distinct and therefore the strategic considerations should be addressed separately. In this chapter five different segments have been identified:

- Toys, for which the final customers are children or young people and the use is educational.
- Hobby/leisure, for which the final customers are young people and adults for recreational uses.
- Professional, for which the final customers are drone pilots and the uses are aerial filming and photography services.
- Commercial, for which the final customers are companies and the uses are agriculture, media, mining, energy, or construction activities.
- Military purposes (vigilance, combat, etc.), for which governments are the end customers.

These segments differ significantly. The price ranges vary widely as well as the basic drone characteristics, like drones with/without a camera, camera quality, flight stability requirements, flight time, data transmission, and so on, so the competitive analysis of the segments must be conducted separately.

Regarding the toy drone subsector, the price is the decisive feature, while quality and technology are not so important. In this segment European companies (mainly from France, UK and the Netherlands) coexist with Chinese ones, whereas North American ones are not represented. Chinese companies offer the cheapest drones (although the French company Parrot offers a minidrone for 30 euros) and have the widest distribution network (not only Amazon but also Aliexpress, which is the most recognized Chinese online seller). To sum up, the companies in this segment follow a cost-based strategy, and Chinese companies seem to have more options. Only by offering distinctive features (for example educational) or additional services (such as competitions for children and young people) can European companies play a role.

The second segment, which we called "hobby", seems to be more interesting for European companies, as quality, reliability, and technology play an important role in the final buying decision. The prices are higher (500–1000 euros); however, although they are important, the prices are not the primary aspect that final users consider when making their buying decision. Technology development (for example allowing the drone to follow you automatically when playing sport, associating with healthy applications, connecting to the usual devices, such as mobile phones or computers, to transfer data and images, and improving the safety measures) are the distinctive features that may define the best players in the near future. Chinese companies coexist with North American and European ones, with no clear leader. The distribution channels, technical support, and after-sales support are named as the key aspects, together with keeping in contact with the regulatory level to comply with safety regulations quickly and safely.

The "professional" segment is experiencing vibrant competition among the European, North American, and Chinese manufacturers. Although the market was led by European companies, the Chinese giant DJI is growing fast, along with other companies, such as Walkera, Zerotech, and Yuneec. The importance of pilot training courses, fair attendance, after-sales and technical support, and the software cost will define the subsector in the near future, together with filming/camera quality and ease of use. The regulations heavily constrain the final users, as they face the need for permits and licences and/or geographical restrictions in carrying out their work properly. The final price still differs by 30–40%, but, as the final characteristics are not especially different, this subsector will tend towards homogenization unless clear quality/technological/service characteristics appear.

The commercial segment has a bright future and is currently the most interesting segment in which to compete. The final prices of drones are high, and the regulations do not particularly affect the final uses, as the main activities are carried out in rural areas or in emergency situations. Most of these drones can be adapted to the final use and associated services, as software and support add value to the final product. European and North American companies are definitely the leaders in this group.

Information regarding the military segment, especially price and distinctive features, is not easy to find. No Chinese company is competing in this segment, and North American and European companies are mainly leading the segment development. The regulations do not affect the development of this segment as heavily, as the defence and civil fields differ in their limits and possibilities. These companies are often targeted directly by governments due to information restrictions, assuring, on one hand, the technological development and, on the other hand, strategic defence and information upgrades.

The easy of entry into the industry and the expansion of the biggest manufacturers, DJI especially, to other segments, is an important threat for companies operating in segments such as professional and commercial. Moreover, this big firm enters the segment with lower prices, forcing the existing companies to reduce their own prices. Companies are also responding to this threat with a value increase of their products, based on their associated software, which has been developed for specific industries (agriculture, mining, etc.). As a consequence, products have become solutions and cooperation between drone manufacturers and software firms has been the trend during the last years. Military companies have also been attracted to the commercial segment, taking advantage of its advanced technology, which can be used in industries other than defence. Despite positive forecasts for the commercial segment in the next two decades, an increase in rivalry might reduce the profitability in the medium term due to the life cycle of the technologies incorporated into the products. Companies will need to adapt their solutions constantly and take care of their customers by supporting them in purchasing, use, and maintenance.

The main difficulty that we faced during the elaboration of this chapter was the lack of statistics related to this sector. The registration of drone operators, including the drones to be operated, would increase the information available for companies, policy makers, and researchers.

References

Agencia Estatal de Seguridad Aérea (AESA) (2017) Registro de declaración responsable de operador de aeronaves RPA's. www.seguridadaerea.gob.es/lang_castellano/cias_empresas/trabajos/rpas/default.aspx. Accessed 22 July 2017

Amukele T, Ness PM, Tobian AAR, Boyd J, Street J (2017) Drone transportation of blood products. Transfus Pract 57:582–588

AUVSI (2016) Maker melting point. Unmanned Syst 34(4):14–15

Casella E, Collin A, Harris D, Ferse S, Bejarano S, Parravicini V, Hench JL, Rovere A (2017) Mapping coral reefs using consumer-grade drones and structure from motion photogrammetry techniques. Coral Reefs 36:269–275

Chabot D, Francis CM (2016) Computer automated bird detection and counts in high-resolution aerial images: a review. J Field Ornithol, 87(4):343–359

Chowdhury S, Emelogu A, Marufuzzaman M, Nurre SG, Bian K (2017) Drones for disaster response and relief operations: a continuous approximation model. Int J Prod Econ 188:167–184

Civil Aviation Authority (CAA) (2017) Small Unmanned Aircraft (SUA) operators holding a valid CAA permission. http://publicapps.caa.co.uk/docs/33/20170714RptUAVcurrent.pdf. Accessed 21 July 2017

Droneii (2016a) Top 20 drone company ranking Q2 2016, activity and global reach of the Top20 leading hard- and software manufacturer in the drone industry. www.droneii.com. Accessed 19 July 2017

Droneii (2016b) Drone company partnership. https://www.droneii.com/drone-company-partner-ships. Accessed 19 July 2017

ENAC (2017) Operatori autorizzati. www.enac.gov.it/La_Regolazione_per_la_Sicurezza/Sistemi_Aeromobili_a_Pilotaggio_Remoto_%28Droni%29/Operatori_SAPR/index.html. Accessed 22 July 2017

Government Office for Science (2017) The UK value stream for remotely piloted civil aircraft systems (RPAS). www.gov.uk/government/publications/value-of-drones-to-the-uk-literature-review. Accessed 22 July 2017

Hardy A, Makame M, Cross D, Majambere S, Msellem M (2017) Using low-cost drones to map malaria vector habitats. Parasites & Vectors 10:29

Hodgson A, Peel D, Kelly N (2017) Unmanned aerial vehicles for surveying marine fauna: assessing detection probability. Ecol Appl 27(4):1253–1267

IAA (2017) Drone operators contact list. https://www.iaa.ie/general-aviation/drones/rpas-aerial-work-permission-holders. Accessed 21 July 2017

Infographic (2016) How tesla developed the first drone ever. https://patentyogi.com/nikola-tesla/tesla-developed-first-drone/. Accessed 17 July 2017

Moe M, Pampoulov L, Jiang L, Franco N, Han S (2016) Eye in the sky. Available via Statista, the statistics portal. www.a2apple.com/eye-in-the-sky/ and https://es.statista.com/estadisticas/660906/prevision-del-valor-mundial-de-los-segmentos-de-mercado-de-drones/. Accessed 17 July 2017

Narkus-Kramer M (2017) Future demand and benefits for small unmanned aerial systems (UAS) package delivery. In: 17th AIAA aviation technology, integration, and operations conference, AIAA AVIATION Forum (AIAA 2017-4103)

Ott I (2012) Service robotics: an emergent technology field at the interface between industry and services. Poiesis & Prax 9(3–4):219–229

Pauner C, Kamara I, Viguri J (2015) Drones. Current challenges and standardisation solutions in the field of privacy and data protection. ITU Kaleidosc: Trust in the Inf Soc (K-2015):1–7

Pulver A, Wei R, Mann C (2016) Locating AED enabled medical drones to enhance cardiac arrest response times. Prehospital Emerg Care 20(3):378–389

PwC (2016) Clarity from above. PwC global report on the commercial applications of drone technology. https://www.pwc.pl/pl/pdf/clarity-from-above-pwc.pdf. Accessed 29 June 2017

Restas A (2015) Drone applications for supporting disaster management. World J Eng Technol 3 (3):316

San Diego Air and Space Museum (2017) http://sandiegoairandspace.org/hall-of-fame/honoree/t.-claude-ryan. Accessed 17 July 2017

Sankey T, Donager J, McVay J, Sankey JB (2017) UAV lidar and hyperspectral fusion for forest monitoring in the southwestern USA. Remote Sens Environ 195:30–43

SESAR Joint Undertaking (2016) European drones outlook study. Unlocking the value for Europe. www.sesarju.eu/sites/default/files/documents/reports/European_Drones_Outlook_Study_2016.pdf. Accessed 19 July 2017

Smith WR (1956) Product differentiation and market segmentation as alternative marketing strategies. J Mark 21(1):3–8

Statista (2016) Nombre d'opérateurs commerciaux de drones déclarés en Australie, au Royaume-Uni, en France et aux États-Unis en février 2016. https://fr.statista.com/statistiques/638340/operateurs-commerciaux-enregistres-monde/. Accessed 5 July 2017

Szantol Z, Smith SE, Strona G, Koh LP, Wich SA (2017) Mapping orang-utan habitat and agricultural areas using Landsat OLI imagery augmented with unmanned aircraft system aerial photography. Int J Remote Sens 30(8/10):2231–2245

Teal Group (2013) Estimated worldwide production value for unmanned aerial vehicles (military drones) from 2013 to 2022 (in million U.S. dollars). Available via Statista, the statistics portal. www.statista.com/statistics/428935/global-production-value-forecast-for-unmanned-aerial-systems-or-drones/. Accessed 5 July 2017

The Guardian (2015a) Major unmanned aerial vehicle (drone) importing countries between 2010 and 2014, by market share. Available via Statista, the statistics portal. www.statista.com/statistics/429100/major-importing-countries-of-drones/. Accessed 5 July 2017

The Guardian (2015b) Major unmanned aerial vehicle (drone) exporting countries between 2010 and 2014, by market share. Available via Statista, the statistics portal. www.statista.com/statistics/429171/major-exporting-countries-of-drones/. Accessed 5 July 2017

Todrone (2016) 1er barómetro del sector de los drones en España. www.todrone.com/wp-content/uploads/pdf/Informe-Barometro-todrone-baja.pdf. Accessed 22 July 201721

Tractica (2016) Global consumer drones revenue from 2015 to 2021 (in million U.S. dollars). Available via Statista, the statistics portal. www.statista.com/statistics/608931/consumer-drone-revenue-worldwide/. Accessed 5 July 2017

Tractica (2017a) Projected commercial drone revenue worldwide from 2015 to 2025 (in million U.S. dollars). Available via Statista, the statistics portal. www.statista.com/statistics/607922/commercial-drone-market-revenue-worldwide-projection/. Accessed 5 July 2017

Tractica (2017b) Projected commercial drone revenue in Europe from 2015 to 2025 (in million U.S. dollars). Available via Statista, the statistics portal. www.statista.com/statistics/607794/commercial-drone-market-revenue-in-europe-projection/. Accessed 5 July 2017

Tractica (2017c) Drones for commercial application. Available via Statista, the statistics portal. www.statista.com/statistics/607897/commercial-drone-market-revenues-in-middle-east-and-africa-projection/; www.statista.com/statistics/607794/commercial-drone-market-revenue-in-europe-projection/; www.statista.com/statistics/607872/commercial-drone-market-revenue-in-latin-america-projection/; www.statista.com/statistics/607769/commercial-drone-market-revenue-in-north-america-projection/; www.statista.com/statistics/607808/projection-of-the-commercial-drone-market-revenue-in-asia-pacific/. Accessed 17 July 2017

Venter P, Wright A, Dibb S (2015) Performing market segmentation: a performative perspective. J Mark Manag 31(1–2):62–83

Wichmann T (2017) Expanding drone operations into Europe. Available via Skyward. https://skyward.io/expanding-commercial-drone-operations-into-europe/. Accessed 21 July 2017

Wind Y (1978) Issues and advances in segmentation research. J Mark Res 15(3):317–337

European Union Policies and Civil Drones

Virginia Santamarina Campos

Abstract This chapter provides an analysis of the drone policies in the European Union, divided into types of actors (manufacturers, operators, and pilots), drones (more or less than 150 kg, risk classification), licenses, and insurance (depending on the drone and the activity), at the European level. All these policies affect producers and operators. The problems related to licenses, the type of drone and activity, and the chance of obtaining insurance will have an impact on the development of the drone industry in the future. According to the European Union, there are two main current recommendations when regulating drone use: (a) distinguish not by mass but by risk (although mass is a parameter to bear in mind) and (b) do not distinguish the use/mission of the drone, since, depending on the drone, the risks can be the same for both professional and hobby/leisure use.

1 Introduction

Many proposals concerning how to classify drones, RPASs (remotely piloted aircraft systems), UASs (unmanned aircraft systems), or UAVs (unmanned aerial vehicles) can be found in specific literature, and a comparison of these can be consulted in, for example, Hassanalian and Abdelkefi (2017). A basic classification first of all distinguishes the mission of the drone: civilian or military. Of course, one question immediately arises in both cases: why employ a drone? The advantages for both civilian and military missions are quite obvious: the "flying robots" are unmanned. Thus, for example in military operations, the injury/loss of a pilot can be avoided. However, this is also true for civilian purposes. The inspection of a bridge can be performed by a drone (RPAS), and no engineer has to climb or abseil for monitoring purposes. Deployment and maintenance are also cheaper, which is another benefit when drones are employed. This has made basic and applied research in the last years attractive for both types of mission, civilian and military.

V. Santamarina Campos (✉)
Universitat Politècnica de València, Valencia, Spain
e-mail: virsanca@upv.es

M. de Miguel Molina and V. Santamarina Campos (eds.), *Ethics and Civil Drones*,
SpringerBriefs in Law, https://doi.org/10.1007/978-3-319-71087-7_3

As a consequence, great technological progress has been achieved, leading to the successful introduction of drones into the mass market with low prices and their use in different sectors, such as leisure, cultural heritage, industrial inspections, agriculture, emergencies, surveillance, transport, health, and so on.

This is reflected in the fact that the drone market has increased exponentially in the last years. As shown in Fig. 1, not only manufacturers but also services compound this sector, in which manufacturers and components comprised 45% in 2016 (platforms 29% and components and systems 16%), while related activities included the remaining 65%, such as services (20%), universities and research programmes (10%), software (7%), news/media/blogs (6%), coalitions/organizations/initiatives (5%), conferences and events (3%), operator marketplaces (2%), drone insurance (2%), and user groups/networks (1%).

On the other hand, new applications can generate a larger market in the coming years, in which the business opportunities can generate a value of more than 127 million dollars (Table 1).

However, this situation entails a legal vacuum, whereby drones fall outside the aviation rules if their weight is less than 150 kg (Regulation CE no. 216/2008), and in this case each Member State of the European Agency of Safety Aviation (EASA) has to define its own parameters (EASA 2015, 2017).

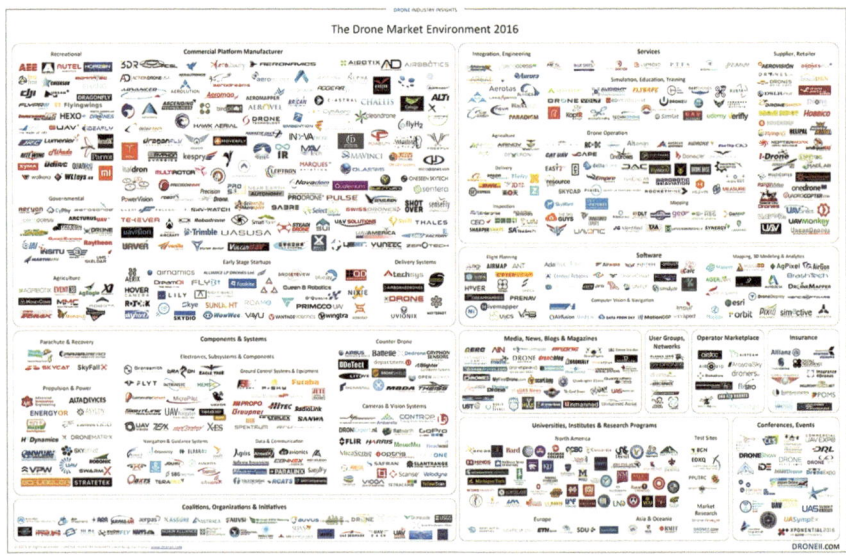

Fig. 1 The drone market environment map 2016, with permission of the company. *Source* Droneii (2016)

Table 1 Value of drone powered solutions' addressable industries: global view ($ bn)

	2015
Infrastructure	45.2
Transport	13.0
Insurance	6.8
Media and Ent.	8.8
Telecommunication	6.3
Agriculture	32.4
Security	10.5
Mining	4.3
Total	127.3

Source PwC (2016)

2 Actors

According to the EASA (2015, 2017), different stakeholders are affected by civil drones: national aviation authorities, the aviation industry, air navigation service providers (ANSPs), airspace users (or pilots), manufacturers, drone operators, and the general public.

In our research five main parties should be taken into account:

- Drone manufacturers: that is, the producers of the final product. They could be from the EU or from a non-EU country. Nevertheless, all of them should comply with the EU country requirements.
- Operators: people holding a license to navigate a drone as well as people who give training to other pilots. That is, their drone use has purely a professional/commercial purpose.
- Pilots/users: they can also be operators when there is professional/commercial use of the drone, but they might also hold no license if the drone weight is below a specific value and is used just for hobby/leisure purposes.
- Members of the general public: their safety and security can be affected by a drone. The main concerns for people are related to safety, the environment, privacy, and data protection (Smith 2014).
- The economy: businesses that may include the use of UASs in their business model to lower costs and/or add new innovative services.

In the case of civil drones weighing less than 150 kg, it is apparent that different European countries regulate the activity of these actors differently. For example, in 2016 the use of camera drones was made illegal in Sweden by its Supreme Administrative Court unless the users have been granted a special surveillance permit (BBC 2016), even though in 2014 more than 1000 permits were issued for the use of camera drones for commercial purposes in this country.

3 European Policies: A Brief Review

The EASA (2015: 4) provided a regulatory definition of a drone, which could be very useful in the case of courts' discrepancies:

> Drone shall mean an aircraft without a human pilot on board, whose flight is controlled either autonomously or under the remote control of a pilot on the ground or in another vehicle.

Moreover, a consultation for this Advance Notice of Proposed Amendment (A-NPA) (EASA 2015) was open until 25 September 2015. This proposal basically distinguished three categories of drones depending on the risks associated with people and property: open (low risk), specific (medium risk), and certified (high risk) (Fig. 2).

- 'Open' category (low risk): this could include indoor drones
- 'Specific operation' category (medium risk): a manual of operations with a list of the risk mitigation measures will be required
- 'Certified' category (higher risk): a licence and approval of maintenance, operations, training, and so on will be required.

Following that proposal, a new one was presented by the EASA in (2017) to create a regulatory framework for the operation of drones in the case of the open and specific categories. This draft was available for enquiry until 15 September 2017. All this information will be used by the EASA to elaborate a comment review document (CRD).

Fig. 2 Changes proposed by the EASA. *Source* own elaboration adapted from the EASA

The European Council and the Parliament are continuing to work together to provide a common regulatory framework to support the European competitiveness and leadership in the drone sector to deliver new employment and business opportunities and, at the same time, to respect safety, privacy, and the environment, as stated in the Warsaw Declaration (EASA 2016).

This new regulatory framework is supposed to be presented to the European Commission by the end of 2017, so at present licences and assurances and types of activities and drones are still regulated differently by the European countries, as we can see in the chapters "Spain-UK-Belgium Comparative Legal Framework" and "Legal and Ethical Recommendations".

However, some countries have started to change their own regulations. For example, in the UK, even with the "Brexit" process pending and without knowing whether that future framework will be applied in this country, in 2017 the Government announced a plan to require the owners of drones weighing more than 250 g to register their devices (TechCrunch 2017). Moreover, a new drone safety awareness test will have to prove that the drone operators understand the relevant safety, security, and privacy regulations.

4   Insurance Regulations and Drones in the European Union

The European Insurance Regulation on the insurance requirements for air carriers and aircraft operators (European Commission 2004) requires them to be insured with some exceptions: among them, these include model aircrafts with a maximum take-off mass (MTOM) of less than 20 kg when used for non-commercial purposes. However, even though there is no definition of what a model aircraft is for the purposes of the European Insurance Regulation, it is assumed that it encompasses drones. Therefore, an operator is exempt from the insurance requirement if he/she uses a drone weighing less than 20 kg for non-commercial purposes (Farrar's Building 2016).

Moreover, article 3 of this Regulation provides the following definition of an aircraft operator:

> ... means the person or entity, not being an air carrier, who has continual effective disposal of the use or operation of the aircraft; the natural or legal person in whose name the aircraft is registered shall be presumed to be the operator, unless that person can prove that another person is the operator.

Furthermore, a commercial operation is defined as "an operation for remuneration and/or hire". Therefore, any purpose that could generate income must be a commercial purpose and require the drone operator to hold insurance; in this sense most commercial uses will be obvious if the drone is being used by a company or organization (Farrar's Building 2016).

5 Conclusions

The drone market has increased exponentially in the last years, and many involved parties depend on drone activities: national aviation authorities, the aviation industry, the general public, manufacturers and operators of drones, air navigation service providers (ANSPs), and airspace users (or pilots). However, at present, without a common regulatory framework, different European countries regulate the activity of these actors in different ways. Those uncertainties hamper the economic development of this big European market.

While in the case of professional and commercial activities the rules seem to be easier to approach (as, for example, in the case of insurance for drones), the regulation of recreational activities might be quite difficult. For this reason the European Agency of Safety Aviation (EASA) is continuing to work to provide a common regulatory framework to support the European competitiveness and leadership in the drone sector, to deliver new employment and business opportunities, and, at the same time, to give other European citizens who could be affected by drones' activity more safety and security.

References

BBC (2016) Sweden bans cameras on drones. http://www.bbc.com/news/technology-37761872. Accessed 18 August 2017

Droneii (2016) The drone market environment map 2016. https://www.droneii.com/drone-market-environment-map-2016. Accessed 7 August 2017

EASA (2015) Advance notice of proposed amendment 2015-10, A-NPA. https://www.easa.europa.eu/system/files/dfu/A-NPA%202015-10.pdf. Accessed 6 July 2017

EASA (2016) Warsaw declaration: drones as a leverage for jobs and new business opportunities. https://ec.europa.eu/transport/sites/transport/files/drones-warsaw-declaration.pdf. Accessed 18 August 2017

EASA (2017) Notice of proposed amendment 2017-05, B-NPA. Introduction of a regulatory framework for the operation of drones, unmanned aircraft system operations in the open and specific category. https://www.easa.europa.eu/system/files/dfu/NPA%202017-05%20%28B%29.pdf. Accessed 18 August 2017

European Commission (2004) Regulation (EC) no. 785/2004 of the European Parliament and of the Council of 21 April 2004 on insurance requirements for air carriers and aircraft operators. Available via EURLEX. http://eur-lex.europa.eu/legal-content/EN/TXT/HTML/?uri=CELEX:32004R0785&from=EN. Accessed 21 August 2017

Farrar's Building (2016) Drones and insurance. http://www.farrarsbuilding.co.uk/insurance-law-update-december-2016/#_ftn2. Accessed 19 August 2017

Hassanalian M, Abdelkefi A (2017) Classifications, applications, and design challenges of drones: a review. Prog in Aerosp Sci 91(May):99–131

PwC (2016) Clarity from above. PwC global report on the commercial applications of drone technology. http://pwc.blogs.com/files/clarity-from-above-pwc.pdf. Accessed 7 August 2017

Smith ML (2014) Regulating law enforcement's use of drones: the need for state legislation. Harv J Legis 52:423–455. https://doi.org/10.2139/ssrn.2492374

TechCrunch (2017) Drone registration coming to the UK. https://techcrunch.com/2017/07/22/drone-registration-coming-to-the-uk/. Accessed 18 August 2017

Spain–UK–Belgium Comparative Legal Framework: Civil Drones for Professional and Commercial Purposes

Miguel Rosa, Gavin O'Brien and Vadim Vermeiren

Abstract The aim of this study is to compare the regulations of the three European countries applied to drones or RPASs (remotely piloted aircraft systems) to find similarities and differences, particularly in the use of civil drones for professional and commercial purposes. This analysis gives a clear understanding of the requirements that each country establishes to operate with drones in its territory. As a general rule, countries regulate the activity of drones in their territory by residents in the country, although they leave the door open to operators from other countries to operate legally. In general, the focus of international and national regulations is given to safety. Nevertheless, small drones avoid many of these requirements, as they weigh less than 150 kg and pose fewer risks to people. However, bearing in mind that this kind of work could be related to creative industries, on a professional level, insurance should cover any property damage.

1 Introduction

Since approximately 2011 there has been an increasing tendency to legislate the use of drones in the civil sphere, countries being incorporated with more or less celerity into a regulatory process that is lengthened by the aeronautical approach adopted. Drones are rated as aircraft and treated as such in the use of airspace and in their relationship with other users, both active (other aircraft) and passive (people who

M. Rosa (✉)
Aerotools, Alcobendas (Madrid), Spain
e-mail: miguel.rosa@aerotools-uav.es

G. O'Brien
Clearhead, Luton, United Kingdom

V. Vermeiren
Pozyx, Ghent, Belgium

© The Author(s) 2018
M. de Miguel Molina and V. Santamarina Campos (eds.), *Ethics and Civil Drones*,
SpringerBriefs in Law, https://doi.org/10.1007/978-3-319-71087-7_4

are outside the scope of use but who may be affected), with a requirement for safety conditions in the operation that are comparable as far as possible to those of manned aviation.

As Bernauw (2016) highlights, Art. 8 of the Chicago Convention (ICAO 2006) subjects the operation of drones to national authorization. The consequence at present is a regulatory environment that differs between the respective countries, from permissive to restrictive, while the professional and commercial use of drones has an impact on safety that must be addressed.

In countries that already have legislation, there is evidence of some homogeneity in some aspects of regulation, as is the case with the weight limits (MTOW, maximum take-off weight) of regulated aircraft, the operation limits (height, distance to the pilot, etc.), or the registration requirements for the operator, although there is no harmonized regulation in common spaces such as the European Union (EU). In this regard the strategy has been defined to achieve common European legislation (towards 2018), and working groups have been established to develop it under the ward of the Council, the European Commission, and the European Parliament, with the EASA (European Aviation Safety Agency) working on drafting legislation.

Bearing in mind that, although there will be a common European regulation, there will always be differences from the regulation of other countries outside the EU. The approach of this study is to attain adequate practical knowledge of the regulation of each country to provide academia with a comparative legal framework as well as to give the user a tool to obtain this information. The parameters analysed are:

- Updated legislation applied in each country;
- Limitations for operating drones;
- Compulsory requirements for operators, drones, and pilots to operate drones.

As a sector that is in the process of settlement and based on technologies that evolve very quickly, it is important to keep in mind at all times that there will be a frequent dynamic of changes and updates of legislation until standardized forms of technology utilization are adopted. For this reason references are included to regulatory agencies and links to the information sources, with the date of the last version of legislation in force.

A table has been drawn up (Table 1) to provide a reference document containing adequate knowledge of the specific legislation. The nomenclature and explanation of the sections are detailed. The table's format tries to parameterize or group the most relevant aspects of each of the regulations under study in sections that are common or at least similar. Although at first glance this is a complicated task due to the different ways of approaching drones' operation, control, and regulation in each country, some common areas have been defined to provide an appropriate guide to be introduced in each piece of legislation.

Table 1 Proposal for a reference document to compare drone regulations related to operators and pilots

	Country	Current regulation
	Parameters	Comments
Administration and regulation		
Regulatory body	Regulatory body name	Link provided in the reference list
Date of last normative update	Date of last normative update	Law that publishes it
Normative identification	Normative name	Link provided in the reference list
Limits to operation		
MTOW (maximum take-off weight)	Value	Maximum take-off mass limit value
Divisions according to MTOW	Value	Value that limits divisions
Maximum flight height	Value	Value
VLOS (visual line of sight)	Value	Explanation of conditions
VLOS—distance to pilot	Value	Explanation of conditions
EVLOS (extended visual line of sight)	Value	Explanation of conditions
BVLOS (beyond visual line of sight)	Value	Explanation of conditions
Number of RPASs piloted by the same pilot	Value	Value
Areas of operation	Description	Explanation if needed
Periods of operation	Value	Explanation if needed
Dangerous goods and substances shipped	Value	Explanation if needed
Flight zones	Aeronautical zone	Requirements
Distance from airports	Value	Explanation if needed
Requirements for the operator (Documentation)		
Registration request	Value (yes/no)	Explanation if needed
Test flight request	Value (yes/no)	Explanation if needed
RPAS characterization sheet	Value (yes/no)	Explanation if needed
Safety study	Value (yes/no)	Explanation if needed
Operation manual	Value (yes/no)	Explanation if needed
Maintenance manual	Value (yes/no)	Explanation if needed
Additional measures	Value (yes/no)	Explanation if needed
Incident notifications	Value (yes/no)	Explanation if needed
Civil liability insurance	Value (yes/no)	Explanation if needed
Requirements according to operators' origin	Value	Explanation if needed
Special permit to operate for foreigners	Value	Explanation if needed

(continued)

Table 1 (continued)

	Country	Current regulation
	Parameters	Comments
Requirements for pilots		
Type of qualification (license)	Type	Explanation if needed
Basic	Value	Explanation if needed
Advanced	Value	Explanation if needed
Practical qualification	Value	Explanation if needed
Requirements	Value	Explanation if needed
Flight/training hours	Value	Explanation if needed
Divisions according to MTOW	Value	Explanation if needed
Medical certificate	Value (yes/no)	Explanation if needed
Language	Value	Explanation if needed
Radiophonist license	Value	Explanation if needed
Requirements for RPASs		
Identification/registration	Element	Explanation if needed
Airworthiness certification	Value	Explanation if needed
Command and control link	Value	Explanation if needed
Maintenance	Type	Explanation if needed
Test flights	Type	Explanation if needed
Requirements for operation		
Previous communication	Value	Explanation if needed
Permission	Value	Explanation if needed
Non-segregated airspace	Value	Explanation if needed
Exceptions	Value	Explanation if needed
Use of RPASs in emergency cases	Value	Explanation if needed
RPAS protection and recovery areas	Value	Explanation if needed
VLOS	Value	Explanation if needed
EVLOS	Value	Explanation if needed
BVLOS	Value	Explanation if needed

Source Own elaboration

2 Regulatory Framework General Evolution

For some years aeronautical authorities have been concerned about the generalization of drones' use, and since 2011 an important effort has been made to integrate these aircraft into the air space with the maximum safety conditions for all users. The problems are the coordination of the different sensitivities and the establishment of a technical scheme suitable for all countries. From the ICAO (International Civil Aviation Organization), coordination is attempted somehow mildly, and the main efforts are exerted through the JARUS organization (Joint

Authorities for Regulation of Unmanned Systems) or through the States within the European Union. Consequently, as it can be seen, different actors influence this regulatory framework, which can sometimes be confusing.

2.1 European Parliament Ruling on Drones

Being aircraft, drones have to comply with aviation safety rules. International civil aviation rules at the United Nations level have prohibited unmanned aircraft from flying over another state's territory without its permission since 1944. In the EU the current regulatory system for drones is based on fragmented rules, with many Member States having already regulated or planning to regulate some aspects of civil drones with an operating mass of 150 kg or less. The responsibility for civil drones of over 150 kg is left to the European Aviation Safety Agency (EASA). However, the extent, content, and level of detail of national regulations differ, and conditions for mutual recognition of operational authorization between EU Member States have not been reached.

In 2012, having completed a set of consultations, the Commission published a staff working document on the civil use of RPASs and established a European RPAS steering group to plan and coordinate EU work on civil RPASs. In 2013 the steering group presented its recommendations in a roadmap that covers all types of RPASs except model aircraft and toys. The roadmap identifies potential improvements to the existing regulatory framework and outlines the research and technologies necessary for the safe integration of RPASs into the EU aviation system.

Subsequently, in 2014 the Commission adopted a Communication outlining a strategy for opening the aviation market to the civil use of RPASs in a safe and sustainable manner. It focuses on how to enable the development of RPASs while at the same time addressing their societal impact. The Commission noted its intention to take a step-by-step approach by first regulating drone operations with mature technologies. More complex operations would be permitted progressively. In the longer term, the objective is to integrate RPASs into non-segregated airspace, which is open to all civil air transport.

2.2 European Aviation Safety Agency (EASA)

The European Aviation Safety Agency (EASA) has been tasked by the European Commission to develop a regulatory framework for drone operations and proposals for the regulation of "low-risk" drone operations. To achieve this, the EASA is working closely with the Joint Authorities for Regulation of Unmanned Systems (JARUS).

Regulation (EC) No. 216/2008 mandates the Agency to regulate unmanned aircraft systems (UASs) and in particular remotely piloted aircraft systems (RPASs) when used for civil applications and with an operating mass of 150 kg or more. Experimental or amateur-built RPASs, military and non-military governmental RPAS flights, and civil RPASs below 150 kg, as well as model aircraft, are regulated by the individual Member States of the European Union.

The EASA has been tasked by the European Commission—following the Riga Conference (held in 2015) and its associated Declaration—to develop a regulatory framework for drone operations as well as concrete proposals for the regulation of low-risk drone operations.

The "Advance notice of proposed amendment 2015-10" (A-NPA) (EASA 2015a) reflects the principles laid down in the Riga Declaration. It follows a risk- and performance-based approach; it is progressive- and operation-centric. It introduces three categories of operations as already proposed in the published EASA "Concept of operations for drones":

- An "open" category (low risk): safety is ensured through operational limitations, compliance with industry standards, requirements for certain functionalities, and a minimum set of operational rules. Enforcement shall be ensured by the police. In this group we could also include indoor drones.
- A "specific operation" category (medium risk): authorization by National Aviation Authorities (NAAs), possibly assisted by a qualified entity (QE) following a risk assessment performed by the operator. A manual of operations shall list the risk mitigation measures.
- A "certified" category (higher risk): requirements comparable to manned aviation requirements. Oversight by NAAs (issue of licences and approval of maintenance, operations, training, air traffic management (ATM)/air navigation services (ANS), and aerodrome organizations) and by the EASA (design and approval of foreign organizations).

This regulatory framework will encompass European rules for all drones in all weight classes. The amendments to Regulation (EC) No. 216/2008 that are underway will reflect the above.

Besides, in December 2015 the Agency published a Technical Opinion (EASA 2015b) that contains, in its section 4, an update of the roadmap published by the European RPAS Steering Group (ESRG) in 2013 (ESRG 2013). This Technical Opinion is the result of the consultation performed with A-NPA 2015-10. It has been developed in parallel to the draft modifications to Regulation (EC) No. 216/ 2008 (hereinafter referred to as the "Basic Regulation") included in the "Aviation Strategy to Enhance the Competitiveness of the EU Aviation Sector" (hereinafter referred to as the "Aviation Strategy"), published on 7 December 2015.

The Agency also supports the work of the ICAO (International Civil Aviation Organization) UAS Study Group. The ICAO published Circular 328 (2011) on UASs and amended Annexes 2, 7, and 13 to the Chicago Convention to accommodate RPASs intended to be used by international civil aviation.

Moreover, the EASA is member of the Joint Authorities for Rulemaking on Unmanned Systems (JARUS), which is currently developing recommended requirements for:

- Licensing of remote pilots;
- RPASs in visual (VLOS) and beyond line-of-sight (BVLOS) operations;
- Civil RPAS operators and approved training organizations for remote pilots (JARUS-ORG);
- Certification specifications for light unmanned rotorcraft (CS-LURS) and aeroplanes (CS-LURS) below 600 kg;
- Performance requirements for "detect and avoid" to maintain the risk of mid-aid collision below a tolerable level of safety (TLS) and taking into account all the actors in the total aviation system;
- Performance requirements for command and control data link, whether in direct radio (RLOS) or beyond line-of-sight (BRLOS) and in the latter case supported by a communication service provider (COM SP);
- Safety objectives for the airworthiness of RPASs ("1309") to minimize the risk of injuries to people on the ground; and
- Processes for airworthiness.

The EASA has already published:

- Guidance material to support approved design organizations (DOA or AP-DOA) in selecting the appropriate certification specifications (among the ones applicable to manned aviation) from which to build the certification basis for RPAS design (see E.Y013-01);
- NPA 2012-10 to transpose amendment 43 to ICAO Annex 2 into the Standard European Rules of the Air (SERA).

2.3   Joint Authorities for Regulation of Unmanned Systems (JARUS)

JARUS is a group of experts gathering regulatory expertise from all around the world. At present 48 countries, as well as the European Aviation Safety Agency (EASA) and EUROCONTROL, are contributing to the development of JARUS's work products. Participation in JARUS is open to all regulatory authorities with expertise in unmanned or remotely piloted aircraft systems.

The purpose of JARUS is "to recommend a single set of technical, safety and operational requirements for all aspects linked to the safe operation of the Remotely Piloted Aircraft Systems (RPAS). This requires review and consideration of existing regulations and other material applicable to manned aircraft, the analysis of the specific tasks linked to RPAS and the drafting of material to cover the unique features of RPAS" (JARUS 2015a).

The JARUS guidance material aims to facilitate each authority to write its own requirements and to avoid duplicate efforts. The work is performed by the JARUS working groups; seven WGs are active at this moment (JARUS 2015b): WG1 Flight Crew Licensing, WG2 Operations, WG3 Airworthiness, WG4 Detect & Avoid, WG5 Command, Control & Communications, WG6 Safety & Risk Management, WG7 Concept of Operations.

In the last three years, it has published and made available to the RPAS community some deliverables to clarify concepts or recommend some uses. It is working to provide further inputs into the development of RPAS and UAS regulatory guidance and recommendations in domains in which other organizations (e.g. the ICAO) have not been active.

JARUS is creating a high-level framework that will be at the heart of the development effort. This effort is based on a number of high-level "concepts of operations" (CONOPS) addressing the key elements of the operation of UASs. These CONOPS set high-level assumptions that should guide the work activities in the coming years. They are aimed at providing a stable yet flexible environment, in which JARUS's work products can be developed and amended as necessary. This will allow innovation to take place with a level of certainty. The members of JARUS have agreed to develop these CONOPS for the following subjects:

- Regulatory oversight with three categories—A, B, and C or open, specific, and certified;
- UAS operational categorization;
- Specific operational risk assessment specifications (SORA);
- ATM concepts for different operations;
- The detect and avoid concept for visual line of sight, extended, and beyond visual line of sight;
- Command and control, from the simplest to the most complex systems.

After JARUS has reached consensus on these concepts, other deliverables—such as operational, technical, safety, and operational requirements and certification specifications—will be derived to support them.

2.4 International Civil Aviation Organization (ICAO)

In the previous section on the AESA, we introduced this United Nations specialized agency. Established by States in 1944, it manages the administration and governance of the Convention on International Civil Aviation (Chicago Convention). The ICAO works with the Convention's 191 Member States and industry groups to reach consensus on international civil aviation standards and recommended practices (SARPs) and policies in support of a safe, efficient, secure, economically sustainable, and environmentally responsible civil aviation sector. These SARPs and policies are used by ICAO Member States to ensure that their local civil aviation operations and regulations conform to global norms.

The ICAO has developed the UAS Toolkit (ICAO 2017) as a guide to assist States that are working on the development of UAS operational guidance, regulation, and enabling operation in a safe manner. This Toolkit provides interesting guidance to take into account, but users should always be aware that it could be updated.

There seems to be a general consensus that unmanned aircraft must be allowed to operate without segregation from other air space users (Bernauw 2016).

3 Legal Framework of Spain

According to Pauner-Chulvi (2016), Spain was one of the first European countries to pass a technical regulation on drones.

At the national level, the body responsible for regulating the activity of drones is the State Agency for Air Safety (AESA), under the General Secretariat of Transport (Ministry of Development). It is the aeronautical authority and is responsible for the supervision, inspection, and management of air transport, air navigation, and airport security (AESA 2017a). In addition, it assesses the risks in air transport safety through threat detection, risk analysis and evaluation, and a continuous process of control and mitigation of risks. It also has sanctioning power over violations of civil aviation regulations.

Within its activity it is responsible for developing the regulation of operations with drones up to 150 kg and for monitoring their compliance and operation. The drone section has been framed within the Aircraft Safety Directorate, with the description of remote control piloted aircraft units (RPASs).

As the first action, Royal Decree-Law 8/2014 was passed on 4 July, giving "approval of urgent measures for growth, competitiveness and efficiency", in which section 6 included the temporary regime for operations with remotely piloted aircraft, drones, weighing less than 150 kg at take-off.

Subsequently, this legislation was processed as a law, Law 18/2014, on 15 October 2014, giving "approval of urgent measures for growth, competitiveness and efficiency" (AESA 2014), which is currently in force. This regulation responded to the need to establish a legal framework that would allow the safe development of a technologically advanced and emerging sector, and from the beginning it was promised that it would be developed in the short term, the Administration being aware that it was a temporary solution that needed to be improved.

This temporary regulation contemplates the different scenarios in which the different aerial works can be realized, depending on the aircraft's weight. Besides, the conditions now approved are supplemented by the general scheme of Law 48/1960, 21 July, on air navigation and establish the operating conditions of this type of aircraft in addition to other obligations.

Legislation on drones in Spain was published in a somewhat accelerated way in July 2014, to alleviate the sense of freedom, reinforced by the lack of information, that had spread among users over the misconception that "if it is not forbidden, it is permitted". With regard to aircraft, such as aircraft flying within certain defined parameters, there had always been legislation, and the use of model aeroplanes for many years, being restricted to a specific environment (that of fans and aeromodelling clubs), had not posed major problems.

However, the appearance of drones and the extension of their use outside the domain of model aircraft increased the number of users and potentially dangerous situations at the same time as a professional activity "sub-sector" was being formed, gaining size on a base lacking legal solidity.

By the end of 2013 and early 2014, a number of incidents involving drones had occurred, which motivated the accelerated position taken by the Ministries of Development, Defence, and Industry and the elaboration of regulations that were presented as "provisional" pending more elaborate and refined legislation.

Royal Decree 8/2014 covered the regulation of RPASs, conforming to a scenario of use that evidenced certain deficiencies but giving the possibility to undertake work and activities using drones in a legal way. Subsequently Law 18/2014 was approved.

In the years afterwards, work was carried out on new legislation to improve the aforementioned and currently in force legislation with a draft that has already circulated in its final versions and that seems only to be waiting for its approval by the Government.

Given the imminence of this new legislation, it has been considered appropriate to include and consider it at the same level as Law 18/2014, which is in force, to achieve adequate knowledge about a reality that seems close, although it must be borne in mind that changes may still be made to the wording of some points of this new regulation. The version has been developed by the Ministry of Public Works and Transport and the Ministry of Defence (2016).

To gain an adequate understanding of the regulation of drones and how it applies, it is necessary to examine the "guidance material" published by the State Agency for Air Safety (AESA 2017b), which articulates the implementation of the law.

3.1   Current Regulation

At the moment the regulation in force is defined by the following parameters (Table 2):

Table 2 Administration and regulation in Spain

	Spain	Actual regulation
	Parameters	Comments
Administration and regulation		
Regulatory body	AESA	AESA: drones less than 150 kg EASA: drones more than 150 kg
Last updated normative	15 October 2014	BOE (State Official Bulletin) 17 October 2014
Normative identification	Law 18/2014 Section 6th Civilian aeroplanes piloted by remote control	Article 50 distinguishes drones less than 2 kg, drones less than 25 kg, and drones less than 150 kg

Source Own elaboration

3.2 New Regulation and Comparison

There is the intention on the part of the Spanish Administration to update the legislation on drones in the short term, and it has elaborated a draft of regulation that is waiting for the last political formalities for its approval and publication.

A comparative analysis of the two regulations is displayed in Table 3. As we can observe, some parameters have no changes, while others are more detailed or adjusted.

4 Legal Framework of the UK

In the UK the administration authority in charge of civil drones is the Civil Aviation Authority (CAA). In relation to drones (CAA 2017a), the regulation separates drones as follows: up to 7 kg or up to 20 kg (small) and up to 150 kg (light). Art. 94 of the Air Navigation Order (CAA 2017b) and the regulations made under the order exclude small drones from some obligations.

However, this depends on the use of the drone. It is not compulsory to register a personal drone or obtain a permit for a recreational drone in the UK, but, if the drone is used for professional work, then a Permission for Aerial Work is needed, which has to be renewed annually (CAA 2017a).

The basic parameters are the following:

- Line of sight (LOS) at a maximum height of 400 ft (122 m);
- 500 m of distance horizontally;
- In any case fly away from aircraft, helicopters, airports, and airfields;
- If fitted with a camera, a drone must be flown at last 50 m away from a person, vehicle, building, or structure not owned or controlled by the pilot;
- Camera-equipped drones must not be flown within 150 m of a congested area or large group of people, such as a sporting event or concert.

Table 3 Comparative analysis of regulations in Spain

	Spain			Spain	New regulation
	Parameters	Current regulation		Parameters	Comments
		Comments			
Administration and regulation					
Regulatory body	AESA			AESA	No changes
Last normative update	15 October 14	BOE 17/10/2014		Pending	
Normative identification	Law 18/2014 Section 6	Article 50		Pending	
Limits for operation					
MTOW	<25 kg			<25 kg	No changes
Divisions according to MTOW				<10 kg	To fly over populated areas; new regulation
Maximum flight height	120 m			120 m	No changes
VLOS	MTOW <25 kg	Keeping control of aircraft at all times from a ground control station (GCS)		MTOW <25 kg	No changes
VLOS—distance to pilot	<500 m	Keeping visual contact		<500 m	No changes
EVLOS		Not allowed		MTOW <25 kg	Observers within 500 m distance from pilot and communicated
BVLOS	MTOW <2 kg	Keeping control of aircraft at all times from a GCS		MTOW <2 kg	No changes
BVLOS				MTOW <25 kg	Mandatory detect and avoid (D&A) system on board or in segregated airspace

(continued)

Table 3 (continued)

	Spain	Current regulation	Spain	New regulation
	Parameters	Comments	Parameters	Comments
Number of RPASs piloted by the same pilot	1		1	No changes
Areas of operation		Non-populated areas or buildings		No changes
		Non-controlled airspace		No changes
			Urban areas and over populated zones	Probably no changes, depending on risk
Periods of operation	Daytime	Always	Daytime/night-time	Specific safety requirement
Dangerous goods and substances shipped	No		No	No changes
Flight zones	Non-controlled airspace	Regular safety study	Non-controlled airspace	No changes
			Controlled airspace or FIZ (flight information zone)	Specific safety study
Distance from airports	>8 km or >15 km with the instrument flight rules (IFR) system	A shorter distance is allowed when agreed and coordinated with airport management	To be determined (TBD)	Agreed and coordinated with airport management—specific safety study
Requirements for the operator (Documentation)				
Registration request	Yes	Declaration	Yes	No changes
Test flight request	Yes	Previous to definitive registration	Yes	No changes

(continued)

Table 3 (continued)

	Spain	Current regulation	Spain	New regulation
	Parameters	Comments	Parameters	Comments
RPAS characterization sheet	Yes	For each RPAS	Yes	No changes
Safety study	Yes	For each scenario	Yes	No changes
Operation manual	Yes		Yes	No changes
Maintenance manual	Yes		Yes	No changes
Additional measures	Yes	To avoid interference	Yes	No changes
Incident notifications	Yes	Mandatory	Yes	No changes
Civil liability insurance	Yes	For each aircraft, €300 k min.	Yes	No changes
Requirements according to operators' origin	Open		Open	No changes
Special permit to operate for foreigners	Open	Official language competency is mandatory	Open	No changes
Requirements for pilots				
Type of qualification (license)	Qualification	Not a license	Qualification	No changes
Basic	50 h	VLOS—on-site and online (with 5 h onsite session) + on-site exam	50 h	No changes

(continued)

Table 3 (continued)

	Spain	Current regulation	Spain	New regulation
	Parameters	Comments	Parameters	Comments
Advanced	60 h	BVLOS—on-site and online (with 6 h on-site session) + on-site exam	60 h	No changes
Practical qualification	For each aircraft	Specific aircraft, almost a type certificate	For each aircraft	No changes
Requirements		On-site theoretical class 5 h + theory exam + practical exam		No changes
Flight/training hours	No		Yes	>3 h in the last 3 months for each category of aircraft
Divisions according to MTOW	<5 kg; <15 kg	To be considered as similar RPASs for qualification	<5 kg; <15 kg	No changes
Medical certificate	Yes	LAPL certificate (light aircraft pilot licence) or class 2 certificate until the LPAL is in force	Yes	LPAL certificate (as for light aircraft manned piloting certificate)
Language	ESP		ESP	No changes
Radiophonist license	No	Current regulation	Yes	For flights in controlled airspace
Requirements for RPASs				
Identification/ registration	Identification plate	MTOW <25 kg	Identification plate	No changes
	Registration	MTOW >25 kg	Registration	No changes
Airworthiness certification	MTOW >25 kg		MTOW >25 kg	No changes
Command and control link		At all times		No changes
Maintenance	Maintenance programme	Provided by the manufacturer	Maintenance programme	No changes

(continued)

Table 3 (continued)

	Spain	Current regulation	Spain	New regulation
	Parameters Previous	Comments	Parameters Previous	Comments
Test flights	Previous	For operator registration, to demonstrate that operation is performed safely	Previous	No changes
Requirements for operation				
Previous communication	Yes	Registration	Yes	No changes
Permission	Yes	Specific and temporary for testing flights	Yes	For flights in controlled traffic regions (CTRs), BVLOS, or populated areas
Non-segregated airspace	Yes	Mandatory	Yes	Mandatory but other scenarios are considered with permission
Exceptions	No	CTR or FIZ flights are not allowed	Yes	CTRs, FIZs, or populated areas
Use of RPASs in emergency cases	Yes	Exemptions are considered in emergency cases	Yes	Specific exemptions are stated for operation in emergency cases
RPAS protection and recovery areas	No	Not allowed	Yes	R >30 m for take-off and landing
VLOS	Yes	MTOW <25 kg	Yes	No changes
EVLOS		Not allowed	MTOW <25 kg	Observers within 500 m distance from the pilot and communicated
BVLOS	MTOW <2 kg	Issue of notice to airmen (NOTAM)	MTOW <2 kg	No changes
BVLOS	2 <MTOW <25 kg	Segregated airspace	2 <MTOW <25 kg	With a D&A system in non-controlled airspace—without a D&A system in segregated airspace

Source Own elaboration and EASA (2017)

It is important to respect "no fly zones", which depend not only on the city or town but also on the commons. For example, in London, London's royal parks, Wimbledon Common, Putney Common, and Clapham Common, among others, are no-drone zones. In other cases, such as the borough of Lambeth, a commercial licence is necessary. Therefore, it is better to check with the local council before flying. There is still confusion in some areas about whether drones are permitted or not.

In the case of private property, it is possible to fly in the airspace above (but not higher than the general rule of 400 ft) as long as it does not cause a nuisance, infringe privacy, or otherwise interfere with the "ordinary use and enjoyment" of the land.

On the other hand, the regulation makes no distinction between indoor or outdoor flights in the case of commercial work. Certain hazard factors are heavily mitigated by the fact that the aircraft is flying in an enclosed environment and access to the venue can be controlled (CAA 2017a).

The UK Government is proposing to change the regulations so that any recreational drone weighing more than 250 g has to be registered. Ministers also want drones to be "electronically identifiable" on the ground so that their owners can be tracked. They are also proposing increases to the maximum fine for flying in a no-fly zone, which is currently limited to £2500.

It is not necessary to have drone insurance by law, but it will protect the operator against claims. Moreover, endangering an aircraft in flight is a criminal offence in the UK, and anyone convicted of the charge can face a prison term. Some drones have the capacity to geo-fence restricted areas, such as airports. They can also be used in "beginner" modes, which limit the height and distance that the quadcopter can fly away from the user.

In Table 4 we can observe the different parameters according to UK regulation. As our first observation, we can notice that the UK regulation is less detailed than the Spanish one reviewed.

5 Legal Framework of Belgium

The Belgian Civil Aviation Authority (BCAA) published the Royal Decree of 10 April 2016 "concerning the use of remote controlled aircrafts in the Belgian airspace", which regulates drone operations. It normalizes both the private and the professional use of drones and introduces a registration obligation for drones, regulates the certificates, and defines the authorized take-off and landing spots for registered drones. Moreover, manufacturers of drones need technical requirements, the delivery of conformity certificates, the drafting of a flight manual and safety analysis reporting, maintenance requirements, flight tests, and so on.

According to the BCAA (2017), we can distinguish five types of operations:

Table 4 UK current regulation

	UK	Current regulation
	Parameters	Comments
Administration and regulation		
Regulatory body	CAA	CAA: drones less than 150 kg EASA: drones more than 150 kg
Last normative update	22 February 2017	Differences between drones up to 7 kg and drones up to 20 kg (small)
Normative identification	The Air Navigation Order 2016	Article 94
Limits for operation		
MTOW	<20 kg	
Divisions according to MTOW	<7 kg; <20 kg	
Maximum flight height	122 m	
VLOS	MTOW <20 kg	
VLOS—distance to pilot	<500 m	Keeping visual contact
EVLOS		Need for special approval
BVLOS	MTOW <7 kg	
Number of RPASs piloted by the same pilot	1	
Areas of operation	Limited	Non-populated areas or buildings (min. 150 m)
		Not closer than 50 m to any person
Periods of operation		Always
Dangerous goods and substances shipped	No	
Flight zones	Non-controlled airspace	Safety study
Distance from airports	Yes	Check no-fly zones (http://www.noflydrones.co.uk)
Requirements for the operator (Documentation)		
Registration request	No	Unless commercial: operator's certification
Test flight request	No	
RPAS characterization sheet	No	
Safety study	Yes	Risk assessment specific to the activity being conducted >20 kg
Operation manual	Yes	Flight plan for the activity being conducted
Maintenance manual	No	
Additional measures	No	
Incident notifications	No	

(continued)

Table 4 (continued)

	UK	Current regulation
	Parameters	Comments
Civil liability insurance	No	Unless commercial: operator's insurance
Requirements according to operators' origin	Yes	Professional or commercial
Special permit to operate for foreigners	Open	
Requirements for pilots		
Type of qualification (license)	Qualification	Drone pilot's commercial licence or >20 kg or BVLOS
Basic		Confirmation of the competencies of the pilot
Advanced	No	Special authorization depending on the activity
Practical qualification	Yes	
Requirements	No	
Flight/training hours	Yes	
Divisions according to MTOW	No	
Medical certificate	No	
Language	EN	
Radiophonist license	No	
Requirements for RPASS		
Identification/ registration	Registration	MTOW >20 kg
Airworthiness certification	MTOW >20 kg	
Command and control link		At all times
Maintenance	No	
Test flights	No	
Requirements for operation		
Previous communication	Yes	Registration (commercial)
Permission	Yes	Commercial
Non-segregated airspace	Yes	Mandatory
Exceptions	No	CTR or FIZ flights are not allowed
Use of RPASs in emergency cases	Yes	Exemptions are considered in emergency cases
RPAS protection and recovery areas	No	Depending on the common
VLOS	Yes	MTOW <20 kg

(continued)

Table 4 (continued)

	UK	Current regulation
	Parameters	Comments
EVLOS		Need for special approval
BVLOS	MTOW <7 kg	
BVLOS	7 kg <MTOW >20 kg	Segregated airspace

Source Own elaboration; EASA (2017), Stöcker (2017)

- Private use: maximum higher than 10 m above a private terrain and the drone—weighing less than 1 kg—must be within line of sight at all times. These flights can only happen during daylight, and they are not allowed for commercial or professional purposes.
- Model aircraft: take-off weight between 1 and 150 kg and used only for recreational purposes above a model aircraft terrain recognized by the BCAA, as specified in the aeronautical information package (AIP). They are not allowed for commercial or professional purposes.
- Class 2 operations: not higher than around 45 m above ground outside controlled airspace and outside cities or communities. Operations can only occur in daylight conditions and the drone—weighing less than 5 kg—must remain within the pilot's LOS at all times.
- Class 1b operations: up to around 90 m above ground outside controlled airspace. Moreover, more than 50 m clear of people and/or goods on the ground. Operations can only occur in daylight conditions and the drone—weighing less than 150 kg—must remain within LOS at all times.
- Class 1a operations: up to around 90 m above ground outside controlled airspace. Moreover, closer than 50 m to people and/or goods on the ground or even over them or around an obstacle closer than 30 m. Operations can only occur in daylight conditions and the drone—weighing less than 150 kg—must remain within line of sight at all times. All operations that are not covered in the previous categories are to be considered as Class 1a operations.

Therefore, only classes 1 and 2 can be used for commercial or professional purposes. This means:

- Registration of the drone at the BCAA;
- A certificate of competence in the case of class 2 (taking a theoretical course and passing a practical skill test with an examiner recognized by the BCAA) or a remote pilot licence in the case of class 1 (a theoretical examination organized by the BCAA and a practical skill test with an examiner recognized by the BCAA);
- An operation manual and risk assessment for class 1;

Table 5 Belgium's current regulation (commercial or professional)

	Belgium	Current regulation
	Parameters	Comments
Administration and regulation		
Regulatory body	BCAA	BCAA: drones less than 150 kg EASA: drones more than 150 kg
Last normative update	None	
Normative identification	Royal Decree of 10 April 2016	Drones are divided depending on their weight into class 2 (up to 5 kg) and class 1 (up to 150 kg)
Limits for operation		
MTOW	<150 kg	
Divisions according to MTOW	<5 kg; <150 kg	
Maximum flight height	45–90 m	
VLOS	MTOW <150 kg	
VLOS—distance to pilot	<50 m	Keeping visual contact
EVLOS	Not allowed	
BVLOS	MTOW <5 kg	Prior authorization (Class 1)
Number of RPASs piloted by the same pilot	1	Not specified
Areas of operation	Limited	Not prohibited zones, danger zones, restricted zones, temporary segregated/reserved areas, etc.
Periods of operation	Daytime	All cases
Dangerous goods and substances shipped	No	
Flight zones	Non-controlled airspace	Safety study
Distance from airports	Yes	
Requirements for the operator (Documentation)		
Registration request	Yes	
Test flight request	No	
RPAS characterization sheet	No	
Safety study	Yes	Only class 1: risk assessment by the operator

(continued)

Table 5 (continued)

	Belgium	Current regulation
	Parameters	Comments
Operation manual	Yes	Only class 1: operation manual drafted by the operator
Maintenance manual	No	
Additional measures	Yes	To avoid interference
Incident notification	Yes	
Civil liability insurance	Yes	
Requirements according to operators' origin	Yes	Class 1a (certificate of conformity for the drone) Class 1b (declaration of compliance made by the operator)
Special permit to operate for foreigners	Open	
Requirements for pilots		
Type of qualification (license)	Qualification	
Basic (class 2)	Yes	Theoretical training + practical skill test
Advanced (class 1)	Yes	Theoretical exam + practical skill test
Practical qualification	Yes	
Requirements	Yes	16 years (class 2) or 18 years (class 1)
Flight/training hours	No	
Divisions according to MTOW	Yes	
Medical certificate	Yes	Class 1
Language	FR or NL	
Radiophonist license	No	
Requirements for RPASs		
Identification/ registration	Yes	
	Registration	MTOW >5 kg
Airworthiness certification	MTOW >5 kg	
Command and control link		At all times
Maintenance	Yes	
Test flights	Yes	

(continued)

Table 5 (continued)

	Belgium	Current regulation
	Parameters	Comments
Requirements for operation		
Previous communication	Yes	Flight notification to the BCAA before start of flight (class 1)
Permission	Yes	Authorization to operate received from the BCAA (class 1a)
Non-segregated airspace	Yes	Industrial complexes, nuclear power plants, military zones, and other special zones cannot be flown over unless otherwise described in the AIP
Exceptions	No	CTR or FIZ flights are not allowed
Use of RPASs in emergency cases	Yes	Exemptions are considered in emergency cases
RPAS protection and recovery areas	No	
VLOS	Yes	MTOW < 150 kg
EVLOS		Not allowed
BVLOS	MTOW <150 kg	
BVLOS	<150 kg MTOW >5 kg	Segregated airspace

Source own elaboration and EASA (2017)

- A declaration made by the operator that the organization is in full compliance with the national requirements for class 1b (starting operations only after receiving confirmation from the BCAA and notifying the BCAA of each drone flight before take-off) and the prior authorization of the BCAA for class 1a (the drone has a certificate of conformity from the BCAA or an equivalent document issued by a civil aviation authority from an EU Member State. If not, one must be obtained prior to requesting authorization);
- Forbidden zones at all times are: all controlled airspaces, prohibited zones, danger zones, restricted zones, temporary segregated/reserved areas, and so on. Industrial complexes, nuclear power plants, military zones, and other special zones cannot be flown over unless otherwise described in the AIP.

The use of completely autonomous aircrafts, that is, unmanned drones that do not allow the pilot to intervene immediately to take control over the flight, remains strictly forbidden.

Other chapters of the Royal Decree include provisions for the communication and control software that is implemented in drone technology, incident reporting obligations, mandatory insurance coverage for drone operators, and references to compliance with the applicable data protection and privacy legislation (in particular for drones with a camera functionality).

Table 6 Comparative analysis from Tables 3, 4 and 5

	Spain			UK		Belgium	
	Parameters	Current regulation Comments	New regulation Comments	Parameters	Current regulation Comments	Parameters	Current regulation Comments
Administration and regulation							
Regulatory body	AESA	AESA: drones less than 150 kg EASA: drones more than 150 kg	No changes	CAA	CAA: drones less than 150 kg EASA: drones more than 150 kg	BCAA	BCAA: drones less than 150 kg EASA: drones more than 150 kg
Normative identification	Law 18/2014 Section 6	Article 50 distinguishes drones less than 2 kg, less than 25 kg, and less than 150 kg		The Air Navigation Order 2016	Article 94 Differences between drones up to 7 kg and drones up to 20 kg	Royal Decree of 10 April 2016	Drones are divided into class 2 (up to 5 kg) and class 1 (up to 150 kg)
Limits for operation							
MTOW	<25 kg		No changes	<20 kg		<150 kg	
Divisions according to MTOW			<10 kg to fly over populated areas, new regulation	<7 kg; <20 kg		<5 kg; <150 kg	
Maximum flight height	120 m		No changes	122 m		45–90 m	
VLOS	MTOW <25 kg	Keeping control of aircraft at all times from a ground control station (GCS)	No changes	MTOW <20 kg		MTOW <150 kg	
VLOS—distance to pilot	<500 m	Keeping visual contact	No changes	<500 m	Keeping visual contact	<50 m	Keeping visual contact
EVLOS		Not allowed	MTOW <25 kg Observers within 500 m distance		Need for special approval		Not allowed

(continued)

Table 6 (continued)

	Spain			UK		Belgium	
	Parameters	Current regulation Comments	New regulation Comments	Parameters	Current regulation Comments	Parameters	Current regulation Comments
BVLOS	MTOW <2 kg	Keeping control of aircraft at all times from GCS	from pilot and communicated / No changes	MTOW <7 kg		MTOW <5 kg	
BVLOS			MTOW <25 kg Mandatory detect and avoid (D&A) system on board or in segregated airspace			Requires authorization	Categorized as Class 1
Number of RPASs piloted by the same pilot	1		No changes	1	Not specified	1	Not specified
Areas of operation		Non-populated areas or buildings	No changes		Non-populated areas or buildings (min. 150 m)		Not prohibited zones, danger zones, restricted zones, temporary segregated/reserved areas, etc.
		Non-controlled airspace	Urban areas and over populated zones		Non-controlled airspace		
			Non-controlled airspace		Not closer than 50 m to any person		Not closer than 50 m to any person
	Daytime	Always			Always	Daytime	All cases

(continued)

Table 6 (continued)

	Spain		New regulation	UK		Belgium	
	Parameters	Current regulation Comments	Comments	Parameters	Current regulation Comments	Parameters	Current regulation Comments
Periods of operation			Daytime-/night-time-specific safety requirement				
Dangerous goods and substances shipped	No		No changes	No		No	
Flight zones	Non-controlled airspace	Regular safety study	No changes	Non-controlled airspace	Safety study	Non-controlled airspace	Safety study
			Controlled airspace or FIZ (flight information zone)—specific safety study	Yes	Check no-fly zones (http://www.noflydrones.co.uk)	Yes	Check
Distance from airports	>8 km or >15 km with an instrument flight rules (IFR) system	Shorter distance is allowed when agreed and coordinated with airport management	Agreed and coordinated with airport management—specific safety study	Yes	Check	Yes	
Requirements for the operator (Documentation)							
Registration request	Yes	Declaration	No changes	No	Unless commercial: operator's certification	Yes	
Test flight request	Yes	Previous to definitive registration	No changes	No		No	

(continued)

Table 6 (continued)

	Spain	Current regulation	New regulation	UK	Current regulation	Belgium	Current regulation
	Parameters	Comments	Comments	Parameters	Comments	Parameters	Comments
RPAS characterization sheet	Yes	For each RPAS	No changes	No		No	
Safety study	Yes	For each scenario	No changes	Yes	Risk assessment specific to the activity being conducted	Yes	Only class 1: risk assessment by the operator
Operation manual	Yes		No changes	Yes	Flight plan for the activity being conducted	Yes	Only class 1: operation manual drafted by the operator
Maintenance manual	Yes		No changes	No		No	
Additional measures	Yes	To avoid interference	No changes	No		Yes	To avoid interference
Incident notifications	Yes	Mandatory	No changes	No		Yes	
Civil liability insurance	Yes	For each aircraft, €300 k min.	No changes	No	Unless commercial: operator's insurance	Yes	
Requirements according to operators' origin	Open		No changes	Yes	Commercial	Yes	Class 1a (certificate of conformity for the drone)

(continued)

Table 6 (continued)

	Spain		New regulation	UK		Belgium	
	Parameters	Current regulation Comments	Comments	Parameters	Current regulation Comments	Parameters	Current regulation Comments
Special permit to operate for foreigners	Open	Official language competency mandatory	No changes	Open		Open	Class 1b (declaration of compliance made by the operator)
Requirements for pilots							
Type of qualification (license)	Qualification	Not a license	No changes	Qualification	Drone pilot's commercial licence	Qualification	
Basic	50 h	VLOS—on-site and online (with 5 h on-site session) + on-site exam	No changes		Confirmation of the competencies of the pilot	Yes	Theoretical training + practical skill test (class 2)
Advanced	60 h	BVLOS—on-site and online (with 6 h on-site session) + on-site exam	No changes	No		Yes	Theoretical exam + practical skill test (class 1)
Practical qualification	For each aircraft	Specific aircraft, almost a type certificate	No changes	No		Yes	Both classes
Requirements		Onsite theoretical class 5 h + theory exam + practical exam	No changes	No		Yes	16 years (class 2) or 18 years (class 1)

(continued)

Table 6 (continued)

	Spain		New regulation	UK		Belgium	
	Parameters	Current regulation Comments	Comments	Parameters	Current regulation Comments	Parameters	Current regulation Comments
Flight/training hours	No		Yes >3 h in the last 3 months for each category of aircraft	No		No	
Divisions according to MTOW	<5 kg; <15 kg	To be considered as similar RPASs for qualification	No changes	No		Yes	
Medical certificate	Yes	LAPL certificate (light aircraft pilot licence) or Class 2 certificate until LPAL is in force	LPAL certificate (as for light aircrafts manned piloting certificate)	No		Yes	Class 1
Language	ESP		No changes	EN		FR or NL	
Radiophonist license	No	Current regulation	Yes, for flights in controlled airspace	No		No	
Requirements for RPASs							
Identification/registration	Identification plate	MTOW <25 kg	No changes	No identification		Yes	
	Registration	MTOW >25 kg		Registration	MTOW >20 kg	Registration	MTOW >5 kg
Airworthiness certification	MTOW >25 kg		No changes	MTOW >20 kg		MTOW >5 kg	
Command and control link		At all times	No changes		At all times		At all times
Maintenance	Maintenance programme	Provided by the manufacturer	No changes	No		No	
Test flights	Previous	For operator registration, to demonstrate that	No changes	No		Yes	

(continued)

Table 6 (continued)

	Spain	Current regulation	New regulation	UK	Current regulation	Belgium	Current regulation
	Parameters	Comments	Comments	Parameters	Comments	Parameters	Comments
		operation is performed safely					
Requirements for operation							
Previous communication	Yes	Registration	No changes	Yes	Registration (commercial)	Yes	Flight notification to the BCAA before start of flight (class 1)
Permission	Yes	Specific and temporary for testing flights	For flights in controlled traffic regions (CTRs), BVLOS, or populated areas	Yes	Commercial	Yes	Authorization to operate received from the BCAA (class 1a)
Non-segregated airspace	Yes	Mandatory	Mandatory but other scenarios are considered with permission	Yes	Mandatory	Yes	Industrial complexes, nuclear power plants, military zones, and other special zones cannot be flown over unless otherwise described in the AIP
Exceptions	No	CTR or FIZ flights are not allowed	Yes CTR, FIZ, or populated areas	No	CTR or FIZ flights are not allowed	No	CTR or FIZ flights are not allowed
Use of RPASs in emergency cases	Yes	Exemptions are considered in emergency cases	Specific exemptions are stated for operation in emergency cases	Yes	Exemptions are considered in emergency cases	Yes	Exemptions are considered in emergency cases
RPAS protection and recovery areas	No	Not allowed	Yes R >30 m for take-off and landing	No	Depending on the common	No	Depending on the common

(continued)

Table 6 (continued)

	Spain			UK		Belgium	
	Parameters	Current regulation Comments	New regulation Comments	Parameters	Current regulation Comments	Parameters	Current regulation Comments
VLOS	Yes	MTOW <25 kg	No changes	Yes	MTOW <20 kg	Yes	MTOW<150 kg
EVLOS		Not allowed	MTOW <25 kg Observers within 500 m distance from pilot and communicated		Need for special approval		Not allowed
BVLOS	MTOW <2 kg	Issue of notice to airmen (NOTAM)	No changes	MTOW <7 kg		MTOW <150 kg	
BVLOS	2 kg <MTOW >25 kg	Segregated airspace	With a D&A system in non-controlled airspace—without a D&A system in segregated airspace	7 kg <MTOW >20 kg	Segregated airspace	<150 kg MTOW >5 kg	Segregated airspace

Source Own elaboration

Excluded from the regulatory requirements of the Royal Decree of 10 April 2016 are (a) drones used only to fly inside buildings (indoor); (b) drones used by the military, customs authorities, the police, coastguard, and so on; and (c) certain types of model aeroplanes solely used for personal/recreational purposes, provided that they meet the strict requirements detailed in the Royal Decree.

As our focus is on the commercial or professional use of drones, we summarize the current parameters in Table 5.

6 Comparative Analysis

See Table 6.

7 Conclusions

As we can observe in Table 6, the differences among European countries regarding the operation of drones are still relevant, diminishing the competitiveness of the European drone industry. However, the future legal framework, as designed by the EASA (2017), will create legal certainty for the industry, especially concerning drone requirements in the case of commercial and professional activities.

Furthermore, distinguishing drones depending on their risk and not on their weight could solve the problems of professionals when working in another European country. As an example, we can observe big differences between countries like Belgium, France, Poland, Spain, Sweden, and the UK, where the national authority's permission is limited to 150 kg, while other countries, such as Denmark, Finland, Lithuania, and Portugal, place the upper weight limit at 25 kg.

References

AESA (2014) Law 18/2014, 15 October, "Approval of urgent measures for growth, competitiveness and efficiency". http://www.seguridadaerea.gob.es/media/4389070/ley_18_2014_de_15_octubre.pdf. Accessed 10 July 2017

AESA (2017a) Drones. http://www.seguridadaerea.gob.es/lang_castellano/cias_empresas/trabajos/rpas/default.aspx. Accessed 10 July 2017

AESA (2017b) Guidance material. http://www.seguridadaerea.gob.es/lang_castellano/cias_empresas/trabajos/rpas/material_guia/default.aspx. Accessed 21 Sept 2017

BCAA (2017) Aviation information leaflet: drone flying. https://mobilit.belgium.be/sites/default/files/resources/files/asil_2017_01_drone_flying.pdf. Accessed 12 July 2017

Bernauw K (2016) Drones: the emerging era of unmanned civil aviation. Zbornik Pravnog Fakulteta u Zagrebu 66(2–3):223–248

CAA (2017a) Unmanned aircraft and drones. http://www.caa.co.uk/Consumers/Unmanned-aircraft-and-drones/ Accessed 10 July 2017

CAA (2017b) The air navigation order 2016 (ANO) and regulations, CAP 393, version 5.2. http://www.legislation.gov.uk/uksi/2016/765/contents/made. Accessed 11 July 2017

EASA (2015a) Advance notice of proposed amendment 2015-10, A-NPA. https://www.easa.europa.eu/system/files/dfu/A-NPA%202015-10.pdf. Accessed 6 July 2017

EASA (2015b) Technical opinion. https://www.easa.europa.eu/document-library/opinions/opinion-technical-nature. Accessed 6 July 2017

EASA (2017) Notice of proposed amendment 2017-05, B-NPA introduction of a regulatory framework for the operation of drones, unmanned aircraft system operations in the open and specific category. https://www.easa.europa.eu/system/files/dfu/NPA%202017-05%20%28B%29.pdf. Accessed 18 August 2017

ESRG (2013) Roadmap. Available via SESARJU. http://www.sesarju.eu/sites/default/files/documents/news/-Roadmap_130620.pdf?issuusl=ignore. Accessed 6 July 2017

ICAO (2006) Convention on international civil aviation (Chicago Convention, original 1944), Doc 7300. https://www.icao.int/publications/Documents/7300_cons.pdf. Accessed 11 July 2017

ICAO (2017) UAS toolkit. http://www4.icao.int/uastoolkit/home/about. Accessed 6 July 2017

JARUS (2015a) Terms of reference. http://jarus-rpas.org/sites/jarus-rpas.org/files/imce/attachments/jarus_tor_v0_4.pdf. Accessed 6 July 2017

JARUS (2015b) Definition and structure of working groups. http://jarus-rpas.org/working-groups. Accessed 5 Oct 2017

Ministry of Public Works and Transport and Ministry of Defence (2016) Royal decree (draft). http://fomento.es/NR/rdonlyres/63ECAE3A-B29E-45A7-A885-D314153883EE/139826/RDRPAS27102016.pdf. Accessed 10 July 2017

Pauner-Chulvi C (2016) The emerging use of civilian drones in Spain. Legal status and impact on the right to data protection. Revista de Derecho Político 95:83–116

Stöcker C, Bennett R, Nex F, Gerke M, Zevenbergen J (2017) Review of the current state of UAV regulations. Remote Sens 9(5):459–485

Legal and Ethical Recommendations

María de Miguel Molina and María Ángeles Carabal Montagud

Abstract European countries have fragmented regulations about the manufacture and operation of civil drones; therefore, European institutions are trying to combine all these regulations into a common one by 2019. Until this common framework arrives, not only law but also ethics can give guidelines to the industry to satisfy national standards as well as users' concerns. The European Aviation Safety Agency promotes the highest common standards of safety and develops common safety rules at the European level. This agency and its national equivalents monitor the activity of producers and operators, but, depending on the size of the drone, this activity could cover regulation measures or ethical recommendations. In this sense the aim of our analysis is to categorize the types of hard–soft regulations that we find in the European Union. Our study is based on a content analysis from four sources of information: scientific papers, policies and regulation proposals from the European Union, the regulation and co-regulation of some European countries, and the self-regulation of some drone companies' associations. In general, few countries have chosen self-regulation as a solution to the problems, although in other economic sectors there are positive experiences. With our results we would like to give advice to the European industry as well as providing academia and policy makers with new insights.

1 Introduction

Different regions and countries in the European Union have diverse ways of regulating their commercial and professional activities. In some regions legal regulation is prominent, and there are different normative tools to regulate every economic activity in a detailed manner (the French model, regulation-centred countries).

M. de Miguel Molina (✉) · M. Á. Carabal Montagud
Universitat Politècnica de València, Valencia, Spain
e-mail: mademi@omp.upv.es

© The Author(s) 2018   77
M. de Miguel Molina and V. Santamarina Campos (eds.), *Ethics and Civil Drones*,
SpringerBriefs in Law, https://doi.org/10.1007/978-3-319-71087-7_5

Therefore, individual freedom and organizational decision making are reduced, because legal regulation covers the majority of cases. This is the case of countries such as Spain or Belgium. On the other hand, other regions develop less regulation but use courts' interpretation more, based on previous experiences (the Anglo-Saxon model, jurisprudence-centred countries), giving more freedom to individuals and organizations but less legal security in some cases. For example, this is the situation of the United Kingdom (UK).

However, in the last years, new hybrid models have proposed joint decision making among companies (self-regulation) or between companies and stakeholders, such as the public administration (meta-regulation or co-regulation). These models enhance reflexion and comparison of the "best practices" to follow some excellent organizations to ensure more ethical decision making when legal regulation cannot cover every single case. Some economic and third-sector organizations, such as videogames or sportive competitions, have developed their own rules or soft law in combination with the public administration.

According to Coglianese and Mendelson (2010: 152), and depending on the tool that we use (self-regulation or co-regulation), the organization's discretion increases or diminishes in a pyramid, from freedom to regulation.

As we saw in the chapter "Spain-UK-Belgium Comparative Legal Framework", the regulation of small drones (less than 150 kg) depends on their national regulations. Safety parameters play a key role in the design of civil UASs or RPASs (unmanned aircraft controlled remotely by a pilot, that is, aircraft controlled by a pilot who is not on board). These parameters apply to the producers and the offer of different services by the operators.

Moreover, drones produce other concerns about their use regarding people's personal data (privacy) (Smith 2015). This is mainly an ethical issue on which policy makers should work with stakeholders (Finn and Wright 2016), especially in the case of micro-drones or indoor drones that do not require a flight licence or training to be used. However, the European data protection regulations serve to reinforce this aspect of drones' use.

According to Stöcker et al. (2017), by 2016 more than 80% of the 65 countries with national regulations legislated about drones for 2 reasons: the increasing technology and high-profile safety incidents. Even small mistakes could result in crashes that threaten the health, well-being, and property of the public (Rao et al. 2016).

By now it seems that the necessity of visual line of sight (VLOS) and the lateral distance of the pilot (normally 500 m) are the main shared parameters. Moreover, the minimum lateral distances to people are in the range of 30–150 m.

Nevertheless, as technology is very difficult to regulate, other tools, such as co-regulation and self-regulation, although soft instruments, are useful alternatives for the manufacturers and operators of civil drones (Stöcker et al. 2017). Therefore, we could classify the best practices that fit better with each type of regulation: legal regulation, co-regulation, and self-regulation.

2 Drones' European Legal and Ethical Framework

As Clarke (2014a: 291) highlights in relation to the drone surveillance sector, "the aviation industry has operated for the last seven decades within the framework provided by an international convention, resulting in considerable similarities across almost the entire world", but "no such cohesive influence exists in the field of …" other regulations, such as for civil drones. Furthermore, he is quite critical of soft forms of regulation, as he underlines that the impact of organizational and industry self-regulation is very limited.

Moreover, "despite its theoretical promise, co-regulation too appears unlikely to satisfy the need. Formal regulation therefore appears to be essential" (Clarke 2014a: 291). He gives examples of other successful sectors, and in Clarke (2016: 153) he shows some co-regulation initiatives that could provide more commitment to the drone sector in the short–medium term, due to the fact that in "co-regulation … industry or user organisations perform regulatory functions within a framework set by a government agency". That is because interaction among stakeholders may produce a consensus on a public policy approach in an area in which there is considerable uncertainty (Freeman and Freeland 2014).

As a starting point, and agreeing with Stöcker et al. (2017), all drone regulations have one common goal: "minimizing the risks to other airspace users and to both people and property on the ground". They propose to analyse the different parts that national regulations cover:

- Technical requirements (regarding the product);
- Operational limitations (regarding the operator: distance to airports/strips, limitations to flying over people, limitations over congested areas, prohibited areas, maximal flying height, visual line of sight, beyond visual line of sight, and so on);
- Administrative procedures (certificates, registration, insurance);
- Human resource requirements (qualification of pilots);
- Implementation of ethical constraints (here they include requirements for data protection and privacy).

Thus, as we can observe, the majority of concerns are related to safety, and they only give ethical concerns in relation to privacy. Safety tests are necessary before marketing a drone, and different key attributes of the product should be checked (Clarke 2014b). However, from our point of view, safety can also be included in ethical limitations. Moreover, different current regulations, at least in the European Union, can cover privacy issues.

Regarding data protection, the current European Directive guarantees rights of access, rectification, erasure, and blocking. In addition, the new Directive and Regulation on Data Protection (to commence at the end of May 2018) include the same standards (European Parliament 2016a, b). However, to apply them, it is essential to inform the subjects. Besides, the necessary storage measures should be adopted when processing, according to the European Union Directive.

As mentioned in the chapter "Spain-UK-Belgium Comparative Legal Framework", the European Union has developed some documents to clarify the regulation of civil drones. The current national harmonization actions undertaken by the EASA define riskless open and riskier specific categories. The main European documents are the following:

- Riga Declaration on remotely piloted aircraft (drones), "Framing the future of aviation", Riga, 6 March 2015 (European Commission 2015).
- EASA (European Aviation Safety Agency). A-NPA 2015-10. Introduction of a regulatory framework for the operation of drones. 31 July 2015 (EASA 2015).
- European Union (2015). Opinion 01/2015 on privacy and data protection issues relating to the utilisation of drones, 16 June. Article 29, Data Protection Working Party, 01673/15/EN WP 231 (European Union 2015).
- Juul (2015) Civil drones in the European Union. PE 571.305. Members' Research Service, European Parliamentary Research Service (Juul 2015).

To reach a common legal framework, the European Union has developed several stakeholder consultations, although no legislation has been approved yet.

Furthermore, in other regions, such as the United States, Kaminski (2016) underlines the efforts of the National Telecommunications and Information Administration (NTIA) at the Department of Commerce to host multi-stakeholder negotiations on consumer privacy around drones for industry self-regulation and co-regulation. Moreover, in some specific sectors, the different stakeholders should be informed of the advantages of using drones. For example, Sandbrook (2015) remarks on the importance of identifying the social risks of drones for biodiversity conservation and how they could be mitigated to ensure good ethical practice and minimize the risk of unintended consequences. Accordingly, self-regulation and co-regulation could be adjusted to the different actors' needs.

Industrial manufacturers and professional users are expected to play a key role and contribute to the decision regarding whether UAVs will be a tool for everyone or just for professionals (Stöcker et al. 2017). Codes of conduct are the most-used self-regulation tool to set rules and standards, such as the promises by companies to regulate themselves in the general interest of society (Laudon and Laudon 2016). Some associations of manufacturers and operators of drones have developed codes of conduct (Arkin 2016) that could also provide guidance to the regulators of in-place legal standards and practices (Freeman and Freeland 2014).

As drones' technology changes fast, new organizations' adoption of drone technologies must be paired with clear articulation of their ethical use and full transparency with the public (Culver 2014). For example, information security seems to have received less attention in regulations. However, some measures could be designed by default (Coopmans 2014) to protect information and information systems from unauthorized access, use, disclosure, disruption, modification, perusal, inspection, recording, or destruction (Braun et al. 2015). Some security concerns include hacking, hijacking, cyber-attacks, or other types of vulnerability. Thus, the encryption of communications among all the devices could permit secure computer–RPAS communication and avoid unauthorized access by third parties. For example, there is the possibility of data anonymization, such as pixels to avoid facial recognition when using a camera (Ruchaud and Dugelay 2015).

3 Drones' National Legal and Ethical Frameworks

Following the analysis of the three European countries involved in the AiRT project, we have compared Spain, the UK, and Belgium. The situation in the different European countries is very similar. Normally co-regulation is used to provide the drones' pilots with practical training, while self-regulation in general is not developed in a specific code of conduct.

The training of drones' operators is a key factor for the industry (Clarke 2016). Requiring operators to be licensed and have insurance can impose standards and ensure safety (Luppicini and So 2016).

As a detailed legal study was undertaken in the chapter "Spain-UK-Belgium Comparative Legal Framework", we focus our analysis on ethical tools (Table 1):

In Spain the National Agency of Aerial Safety (AESA) works with different organizations to provide pilots with practical training. In this sense authorization for training is given to (AESA 2017):

- Drone manufacturers
- Organizations authorized by a drone manufacturer
- Licensed operators with their own pilots
- Authorized training organizations (ATOs).

After the training and its assessment (as described by the AESA), these organizations have to send the Agency a dossier containing all the required official documents. This certificate should specify the drone type and model that the person is able to pilot. The certificate it is not necessary in all cases, although it could add value in the case of professional work. Moreover, licensed pilots normally contract insurance, and this constitutes another trust guarantee.

Table 1 Co-regulation and self-regulation initiatives in Spain, the UK, and Belgium

	Spain	UK	Belgium
Regulatory body	AESA	CAA	BCAA
Normative identification	Law 18/2014 Section 6	The Air Navigation Order 2016 (Article 94)	Royal Decree of 10 April 2016
Co-regulation	AESA (practical training)	CAA (permissions for small drone operators)	BCAA (practical training)
Self-regulation	AEDRON	ARPAS-UK	BeUAS

Source Own elaboration

On the side of self-regulation, even though the Spanish Association of RPAS (AERPAS) is the biggest companies' association as it includes manufacturers and operators, it has no code of conduct. There is a smaller association, AEDRON (2016), the Spanish Association of Drones and Similar, just for operators, which has developed one. According to it, some interesting points that the regulation does not cover are:

- To help other pilots in the case of necessity;
- To identify the environmental impacts of the activity in order to minimize them;
- To use biodegradable materials and recycle them correctly;
- To sign the operation's zone correctly.

In the UK, as well as in the previous case, the Civil Aviation Authority (CAA) does not provide training but gives this task to the national qualified entities (NQEs) to assess the competence of people operating small unmanned aircraft (CAA 2015). That is the standard permission to conduct commercial operations with a small unmanned aircraft (drone) weighing 7 kg or less.

Regarding self-regulation, the Association of RPAs (ARPAS-UK 2017) has its own code of conduct. The code, which is very brief and general, is built on three specific themes: safety, professionalism, and respect. Nevertheless, some of its statements could be useful:

- To report incidents to the police, national authority, or relevant industry body;
- To ensure that RPASs will be piloted by individuals who are properly trained and competent to operate the aircraft or its systems;
- To ensure that RPAS flights will be conducted only after a thorough assessment of the risks associated with the activity. Reliability, performance, and airworthiness are established standards.

The case of Belgium is the same. The Belgium Civil Aviation Authority (BCAA) does not provide training, but the Direction Générale Transport Aérien (DGTA) gives this competence to certain organizations (approved training organizations—ATOs). According to article 35 of the Royal Decree of 10 April 2016 on the use of unmanned aircraft in Belgian airspace, the candidates for the position of instructor must meet the following prerequisites:

- Hold a valid remote pilot license;
- Have completed a teaching and learning course;
- Have flight experience of at least 100 h as a remote pilot.

A flight instructor candidate who meets the previous cumulative conditions must pass a practical examination before becoming an RPAS examiner designated by the DGTA. The RPAS flight instructor rating is valid for a period of three years (SPF Mobilité et Transports 2015).

Concerning self-regulation, the BeUAS—La Fédération Belge de l'Aviation Télépilote or Belgian Unmanned Aircraft System Association—just provides a "Charter" (BeUAS 2017) containing a few ethical principles. Among them, we highlight the following:

- Always fly over people with permission;
- Always bear in mind the type or class of drone in use;
- Do not fly a drone at night;
- Respect the operating manual at all times if applicable, knowing the drone's limits and adapting the flight in function.

To sum up, we can observe that self-regulation is focused on operators and the main concerns regarding the ethical aspects of their work are the following:

- To work in a helpful environment, prioritizing safety all the time;
- To minimize the environmental impacts;
- To give all the necessary information and request permission to the people affected by the activity;
- To report incidents;
- To pilot when there is the competence and training to do so in a safe way, respecting the operating manual;
- To analyse the risks associated with the activity, bearing in mind the class of drone in use and the limits.

We think that these measures are in line with the draft of the new European Union regulation but could be useful while that regulation is being approved and implemented.

4 Industry Perceptions

We conducted focus groups in Spain, the UK, and Belgium during February 2017 to contrast with the creative industry the concerns about safety and security when using civil drones for their work. Each group was formed by six to seven expert informants from different sectors, and half of them have a pilot drone license. In total we collected information from twenty people.

The participants attribute the most importance to the experience of the pilot, particularly regarding professional work. For them, trust can be gained when there is training and insurance to cover any eventuality. Additionally, an encrypted Wi-Fi connection is necessary in all cases to give information to the subjects when recording.

Furthermore, the role of the producers is more focused on default measures and giving advice and instructions to the operators.

5 Conclusions

From our point of view, manufacturers and operators are different actors, even though the traditional way of distinguishing standards is to categorize them into active and passive measures all together for both groups. Manufacturers are key actors, as they develop safety and security measures, but operators can just use them, so they are less involved in the design of the product. Manufacturers should work with operators and other stakeholders to improve those measures, because knowing actors' concerns can add considerable value to the product.

Manufacturers could be more centred on safety by default and security by default in designing drones to avoid risky situations in their use. Operators should have the appropriate training to avoid any risk, even for small drones. Maybe if the industry is able to develop very precise drones, the pilots could be inexperienced, but at this moment we think that these cases should be reduced to indoor environments where the risks can be better assessed.

Even if ethics and codes of conduct can help manufacturers and operators of drones, co-regulation whereby public agencies could give some kind of certificate would be an additional element to reinforce other kinds of work in which flight licenses are not compulsory.

As we have observed, in the European countries, co-regulation now is only centred on operators and practical training. The participation of other stakeholders to ensure safety and security is not included. However, other agencies could be involved in the industry, for example to ensure information security, product safety, or data protection by applying different best-practice standards.

Moreover, on the side of regulation, and following Rao et al. (2016: 89), the introduction of compulsory specific insurance could be helpful to create a registry of devices to link each drone to its owner and to help to assign responsibility for illegal activities. On the same line, Boucher (2016: 1409) stresses that citizens see drone regulations as analogous to car regulations; therefore, they should have "mandatory licensing, registration of devices, and mandatory third-party insurance". For him the current focus on public acceptance of civil drone development will move to the development of civil drones that are acceptable to society.

The European Union (2015) recommends that producers can help by giving advice on their packaging and using codes of conduct to self-regulate the industry. Other tools, such as impact assessment or the participation of a Data Protection Officer, could improve clients' reliability. The industry could be proactive in case regulation is not enough.

References

AEDRON (2016) Code of conduct. https://www.aedron.com/codigo-etico. Accessed 18 July 2017
AESA (2017) Practical training, authorised organizations. http://www.seguridadaerea.gob.es/LANG_EN/cias_empresas/trabajos/rpas/req_pilotos/quien_form_practica.aspx. Accessed 18 July 2017
Arkin RC (2016) Ethics and autonomous systems: perils and promises. Proc IEEE 104(10): 1779–1781
ARPAS-UK (2017) Code of conduct. https://www.arpas.uk/mem-code-of-conduct/. Accessed 17 July 2017

BeUAS (2017) BeUAS charter. https://www.beuas.be/fr/membership/beuas-charter. Accessed 20 July 2017

Boucher P (2016) "You wouldn't have your granny using them": drawing boundaries between acceptable and unacceptable applications of civil drones. Sci Eng Ethics 22:1391–1418

Braun S, Friedewald M, Valkenburg G (2015) Civilizing drones: military discourses going civil? Sci Technol Stud 28(2):73–87

CAA (2015) Guidance on using small drones for commercial work. https://www.caa.co.uk/Commercial-industry/Aircraft/Unmanned-aircraft/Small-drones/Guidance-on-using-small-drones-for-commercial-work/. Accessed 18 July 2017

Clarke R (2014a) The regulation of civilian drones' impacts on behavioural. Comput Law Secur Rev 30(3):286–305

Clarke R (2014b) Understanding the drone epidemic. Comput Law Secur Rev 30(3):230–246

Clarke R (2016) Appropriate regulatory responses to the drone epidemic. Comput Law Secur Rev 32(1):152–155

Coglianese C, Mendelson E (2010) Meta-regulation and self-regulation. In: Baldwin R, Cave M, Lodge M (eds) The Oxford handbook of regulation. Oxford University Press, Oxford, pp 146–168

Coopmans C (2014) Architecture requirements for ethical, accurate, and resilient unmanned aerial personal remote sensing. In: 2014 International Conference on Unmanned Aircraft Systems (ICUAS), pp. 1–8

Culver KB (2014) From battlefield to newsroom: ethical implications of drone technology in journalism. J Mass Media Ethics Explor Quest Media Moral 29(1):52–64

European Aviation Safety Agency (EASA) (2015) Advance notice of proposed amendment 2015-10, A-NPA. https://www.easa.europa.eu/system/files/dfu/A-NPA%202015-10.pdf. Accessed 6 July 2017

European Commission (2015) Riga Declaration on remotely piloted aircraft (drones) "Framing the future of aviation". https://ec.europa.eu/transport/sites/transport/files/modes/air/news/doc/2015-03-06-drones/2015-03-06-riga-declaration-drones.pdf. Accessed 18 July 2017

European Parliament (2016a) Directive (EU) 2016/680 of the European Parliament and of the Council, of 27 April 2016, on the protection of natural persons with regard to the processing of personal data by competent authorities for the purposes of the prevention, investigation, detection or prosecution of criminal offences or the execution of criminal penalties, and on the free movement of such data, and repealing Council Framework (Decision 2008/977/JHA). Accessible via EUR-LEX. http://eur-lex.europa.eu/legal-content/EN/TXT/?uri=uriserv:OJ.L_.2016.119.01.0089.01.ENG. Accessed 18 July 2017

European Parliament (2016b) Regulation (EU) 2016/679 of the European Parliament and of the Council, of 27 April 2016, on the protection of natural persons with regard to the processing of personal data and on the free movement of such data, and repealing Directive 95/46/EC (General Data Protection Regulation). Accessible via EUR-LEX. http://eur-lex.europa.eu/eli/reg/2016/679/oj. Accessed 18 July 2017

European Union (2015) Opinion 01/2015 on privacy and data protection issues relating to the utilisation of drones. Article 29 Data Protection Working Party, 01673/15/EN WP 231. Accessible via the European Commission. http://ec.europa.eu/justice/data-protection/index_en.htm. Accessed 18 July 2017

Finn RL, Wright D (2016) Privacy, and ethics for civil drone practice: a survey of industry, regulators and civil society organisations. Comput Law Secur Rev 32(4):577–586

Freeman PK, Freeland RS (2014) Politics & technology: U.S. policies restricting unmanned aerial systems in agriculture. Food Policy 49(1):302–311

Juul M (2015) Civil drones in the European Union. PE 571.305. Members' Research Service, European Parliamentary Research Service. Accessible via European Parliament. http://www.europarl.europa.eu/RegData/etudes/BRIE/2015/571305/EPRS_BRI(2015)571305_EN.pdf. Accessed 18 July 2017

Kaminski ME (2016) When the default is no penalty: negotiating privacy at the NTIA. Denver Univ Law Rev 93(4):925–949

Laudon KC, Laudon JP (2016) Management information systems: managing the digital firm. Pearson, Harlow

Luppicini R, So A (2016) A technoethical review of commercial drone use in the context of governance, ethics, and privacy. Technol Soc 46:109–119

Rao B, Gopi AG, Maione R (2016) The societal impact of commercial drones. Technol Soc 45:83–90

Ruchaud N, Dugelay JL (2015) Privacy protection filter using StegoScrambling in video surveillance. In: CEUR workshop proceedings, vol 1436. http://ceur-ws.org/Vol-1436/Paper62.pdf. Accessed 18 July 2017

Sandbrook C (2015) The social implications of using drones for biodiversity conservation. Ambio 44(4):636–647

Smith ML (2015) Regulating law enforcement's use of drones: the need for state legislation. Harv J Legis 52(2):423–454

Stöcker C, Bennett R, Nex F, Gerke M, Zevenbergen J (2017) Review of the current state of UAV regulations. Remote Sens 9(5):459–485

SPF Mobilité et Transports (2015) Instructeur ou examinateur RPAS. https://mobilit.belgium.be/fr/transport_aerien/drones/instructeur_ou_examinateur_rpas. Accessed 20 July 2017

Conclusions

Virginia Santamarina Campos and Stephan Kröner

Abstract This final chapter exposes the main conclusions of the book and gives some general brief guidelines to the different actors that could be of interest in the drone sector.

1 European Policies for the Drone Sector

At present no common regulatory framework for different European countries exists; thus, each one regulates the activity of drone stakeholders differently. However, it can be stated that a legal framework is possible in the near future, thanks to the European Agency of Safety Aviation (EASA) in cooperation with the industries concerned.

In the case of the employment of drones for professional and commercial activities, it is highly expected that those regulations will help to increase this incipient sector while at the same time ensuring the safety and security of all European citizens who could be affected by drone activities.

2 European Drone Industry

Although the sector has both technological and economic importance in Europe, there are substantial barriers that are preventing it from expanding. As for any industrial development, (over) regulation can be one of the biggest barriers to overcome. In the case of Europe, a conglomerate of independent countries with a common European market, with scattered non-uniform regulations, this might be

V. Santamarina Campos (✉) · S. Kröner
Universitat Politècnica de València, Valencia, Spain
e-mail: virsanca@upv.es

© The Author(s) 2018
M. de Miguel Molina and V. Santamarina Campos (eds.), *Ethics and Civil Drones*,
SpringerBriefs in Law, https://doi.org/10.1007/978-3-319-71087-7_6

even more relevant. It is obvious that, in the case of drones, two important considerations that limit their use have to be taken into account: security/ethical issues and safety. Only if Europe is able to solve these issues quickly and with concise and easy-to-understand policies, while maintaining European standards, will the European industries have the possibility to compete with the big global players from the USA and China. This will not just give an impulse to the European industries (and in particular SMEs) but will also have a considerable impact in the fields of academic, technological, business, and social development.

Although a big part of the evolution of the drone industry has occurred in the last years, led mainly by military needs, nowadays the most innovative drone use is also associated with collaboration (health and drugs delivery, emergency surveillance, security, etc.) and commercial efficiency (agriculture, topography, etc.).

We have distinguished among the different segments within the drone industry as end users. Since their needs and characteristics are totally different, their strategies should be considered separately. In the chapter "The Drone Sector in Europe" five different segments were identified:

- Toys, for which the final customers are children or young people and the use is educational.
- Hobby/leisure, for which the final customers are young people and adults and the drones are designed for recreational uses.
- Professional, for which the end users are drone pilots and the drones are employed for aerial filming and photography services.
- Commercial, for which the final customers are companies that use drones for agriculture, media, mining, energy, or construction activities.
- Military purposes (vigilance, combat, etc.), for which governments are the final customers.

The professional segment is facing vibrant competition among the European, North American, and Chinese manufacturers. Although the market was led by European companies, the Chinese giant DJI is growing fast, followed by other companies. As previously shown, the regulations are heavily constraining the end users, as they are confronting the need for permits and licences and/or geographical restrictions to carry out their work properly. Thus, the corresponding European organism needs to achieve a common agreement for all European countries as soon as possible to maintain and improve competitiveness. If this is achieved, the commercial segment could have a much brighter future than has been foreseen up to now. Regulations do not always affect the final prices (in the case of drones) so much, but on the other hand they provide legal certainty, which is very important for companies, investors, or insurers. This is especially true for indoor use, while outdoor regulations do not particularly affect the behaviour of the end user, since the main activities are carried out in rural areas or in emergency situations. Most of these drones can be easily adapted for a specific purpose, and associated services, like software and support, add value to the final product. In this area European and North American companies are the leaders in this group.

3 Current Legal Frameworks

The differences among European countries in relation to the operation of drones are still relevant, lowering the competitiveness of the European drone industry. However, the future legal framework, as designed by the EASA, will give the industry legal certainty and reassurance, especially in the case of commercial and professional activities. Distinguishing drones by their risk and not by their weight could solve the issues encountered by professionals when working in other European countries.

Moreover, it could be helpful to introduce compulsory specific insurance to create a registry of devices and link each drone to its owner to ensure that responsibility can be clearly assigned for illegal activities (not only in the case of professional drones or drones with a weight of more than 20 kg).

Delving deeper into the matter and talking to the implied industry players, we realized that their main concern about indoor drone use is that professional work needs to be very accurate and therefore piloting experience is necessary. Likewise, indoor environments should be safer for the people affected by a drone's work and drone control should be easy if certain licenses and insurance measures could be applied in all the European countries.

4 Ethical Recommendations

Manufacturers are key actors, as they develop safety and security measures, while operators, as end users, are less involved in the product design. Nevertheless, manufacturers should work together not only with operators but also with other stakeholders to improve those measures, because knowing actors' concerns can add considerable value to the product.

Manufacturers could integrate more safety and security by default when designing drones, avoiding improper and risky use. Operators should receive appropriate training to avoid any kind of risk, even when it comes to navigating small-sized drones. Although ethics and codes of conduct can help manufacturers and operators of drones, co-regulation whereby public agencies could give some kind of certificate could be an additional element to reinforce work situations in which flight licenses are not compulsory.

In the European countries, co-regulation is currently only centred on operators and practical training. The participation of other stakeholders to ensure safety and security is not included. However, other agencies could be involved in the industry, for example to ensure information security, product safety, or data protection by applying different best-practice standards.

The European Union recommends that producers can help by giving advice on their packaging and using codes of conduct to self-regulate the industry. Other tools, such as impact assessment or the participation of a Data Protection Officer, could improve clients' reliability. As a conclusion, the industry could be proactive in case regulation is not enough.

Index

© The Editor(s) (if applicable) and The Author(s) 2018
M. de Miguel Molina and V. Santamarina Campos (eds.), *Ethics and Civil Drones*,
SpringerBriefs in Law, https://doi.org/10.1007/978-3-319-71087-7